If you can add,
subtract, multiply
and divide,
then you can ...

Manage Your Own Financial Future!

A complete, personal financial planning "learning-system" approach to investing

Manage Your Own Financial Future!

This publication contains the opinions and ideas of its authors and is designed to provide useful advice and guidance with regard to the subject matter covered. The author and publisher are not engaged in rendering legal, accounting or other professional services in this publication and cannot address all circumstances unique to each investor and each investment. Laws vary from state to state, as do the facts and circumstances of various investment opportunities and the investor. If legal advice or other assistance is required for particular circumstances, the services of competent professional persons should be sought.

The author and publisher and respective owners, directors, officers and employees expressly disclaim responsibility for any liability, loss or risk, personal or otherwise, which is incurred as a consequence, directly or indirectly, from the use and application of any of the contents of this publication.

The data contained in this publication were obtained from sources believed to be reliable, however accuracy is not guaranteed.

Vesmark, Inc., P.O. Box 16366, Pittsburgh, PA 15242

ISBN 0-9650293-0-1

Printed in the United States of America

How to Order

Copies may be ordered, singly or in bulk, by calling BookCrafters order department at 1-800-879-4214. Quantity discounts are available.

Contents

Module 9 Financial Goals, Portfolio Construction and Preparing Financial Statements 133

Acknowledgements

Vesmark, Inc. wishes to thank the following individuals and organizations for their dedication and expertise. Their knowledge and creativity have added immeasurably to the ultimate quality of this book and we are most grateful for their efforts.

Financial Expertise and Technical Consulting

David M. Cordell, PhD, CFA, CFP, CLU
Associate Professor of Finance
The American College
Bryn Mawr, PA 19010-2196

William J. Ruckstuhl, CLU, ChFC
Associate Professor of Finance
The American College
Bryn Mawr, PA 19010-2196

Lynn Hayes
Assistant Director of Editorial Services
The American College
Bryn Mawr, PA 19010-2196

Executive Editor, Graphic Design, Layout and Preproduction

Adam, Filippo & Associates
Identity & Marketing Consultants
1206 Fifth Avenue
Pittsburgh, PA 15219

We also wish to thank Ibbotson Associates, Inc.,Value Line Publishing, Inc., and the publishers of *The Wall Street Journal* for permission to reprint materials in this book which are under their respective copyrights. These materials were extremely useful in illustrating the concepts presented in this text. Reprinted materials are accompanied throughout by the appropriate copyright notice.

Preface

Would you like to feel more confident about your financial future? More secure about how you manage your finances? Armed with the knowledge you need to reach your financial goals?

Then **Manage Your Own Financial Future!** is for you. Whether you have just started working, have been employed for years, or are ready for retirement, this system will work for you. It is a learning system of financial planning and investment technology. Fresh, exciting, and dynamic, the system unlocks new levels of comprehension and shows you how you can effectively plan and manage your financial future.

You don't have to be an expert in all the fine points of financial planning to do a good job for yourself. What you'll need to know before you start is basic arithmetic–how to add, subtract, multiply and divide. The rest of what you need–a solid foundation in investments, taxation, economics, and finance–the book teaches you. We show you how to connect the relevant parts of these different disciplines so that you can maneuver your way through changing economic conditions and have the information and skills you need to make informed, productive decisions.

How does our financial planning system work? It works through the process of synergy; that is, the individual parts of the system work together (or cooperate) to produce a whole that is greater than the sum of its parts. From a nonsynergistic standpoint, one plus one equals two. However, with synergy, one plus one could equal three, four, five .... When we combine parts that work together, that cooperate, the resulting output can exceed the initial input. This synergistic approach is the basis for our financial planning system.

To support the synergistic approach, we've made the book modular in design. The modules, combined with your active learning participation, are what create a powerful synergy. After reading all nine modules, your knowledge will increase not just nine times, but 15, 20, perhaps even 30 times!

We're not interested in merely teaching abstract theories; we leave that to the textbooks. We are, however, committed to helping you understand enough about financial planning (through the five-step economic model we introduce in Module 3) so that you can make informed, practical decisions about spending, saving and investing money in ways that help you create a secure financial future. This book teaches you how to take charge of your financial future by tying ideas to a real-world model and by supporting those ideas with carefully designed tables, graphs, and charts. We clearly show you how to apply the concepts to your personal circumstances.

Unlike many "Annual Guides to ..." that appear each year at your local booksellers, this book was not written overnight. In fact, years of researching and studying the pre- and post-World War II economy and financial markets have gone into it. But before you get the idea that it's going to take you years to understand what's in it ... let us reassure you. We've made it easy to understand the economic concepts inherent in successful long-term financial planning. And we walk you through the financial planning process one step at a time, so that you can really apply the concepts to your own financial planning activities.

Just as this book was not written overnight, neither should it be read overnight. It is a book of concepts... and concepts often take patience and concentration to comprehend. Many financial planning books today are merely mini-warehouses stuffed full of information that leads nowhere. This book is different. We believe that knowledge without successful application is comparable to a long-distance swimmer who never reaches land. His endless strokes exhaust him, but take him no place... and he is never rewarded by achieving his goal.

We wanted to ensure that anyone could learn to use this system productively, so we've incorporated a powerful new approach to learning to help promote that. Truly understanding what you read so that you can apply your newfound knowledge will take a little patience and concentration on your part. The results are worth it! Like the swimmer willing to persist, what he needs is first to be headed in the right direction and then to be helped to stay on course. We've incorporated the kind of foundation information that will deepen and broaden your understanding so that you can stay on course. And we've made the system a true "learning system" that you can use throughout your lifetime to manage your financial future.

Our "learning-system" approach, *Synergistic Modular Association*℠, promotes learning through synergy, modules of information and the process of association. Each of the nine modules in our system is self-contained, yet structured so that the information in one module can be interconnected with the information in the other modules.

By absorbing one concept at a time and then relating it to the next, you'll truly master the concepts and financial planning methodology we're presenting. You'll see the mystique of financial planning fall away and the reality become clear. What you will be learning all ties together... and it has immediate, real-life application for you!

To be able to use the system, it's important that you read every module, and you must read the modules in order. Each module leads logically to the next, and each builds on what you have learned in the previous module. There is no extraneous information... what's in each module is essential... and it is all interconnected.

If you find yourself getting tired, or discouraged while reading, STOP... take a break, *but don't give up!* Get back to it as soon as you can. You can stop and start within a module as many times as you want. If you have trouble, find someone with whom to share the difficult parts. Shared learning boosts understanding.

There's no magic elixir we can swallow to make us financial planning experts. If there were, we'd all be wealthy, starting with the person who invented the concoction. So, be realistic about setting your reading goals. Pace yourself. Start and stop as time permits. Just don't forget to start again. And make it a priority to finish reading this entire book, *no matter what!* That commitment is your first step in successfully managing your financial future. We wish you success and good fortune!

Vesmark™
The Mark of Financial Planning Excellence™

Manage Your Own Financial Future!

A complete, personal financial planning "learning-system" approach to investing

Module 1 The Power of Compounding

Successful financial planning requires an in-depth understanding of the power of compounding. Therefore, we will begin this module by explaining how to identify when the compounding process is at work.

Multiplication versus Addition

When dealing with annual rates of return on an investment or increases in living costs due to inflation, few people realize that these annual rates are *not* added together; they are *multiplied.* For example, if a $10,000 investment earned a 6% after-tax return each year during a three-year period, the total return would be determined by increasing the beginning investment amount by 6% each year–that is, multiplying by 1.06. At the end of year 1, $10,000 would increase to $10,600 ($10,000 x 1.06). By the end of year 2, $10,600 would increase to $11,236 ($10,600 x 1.06). By the end of year 3, $11,236 would increase to $11,910 ($11,236 x 1.06). The increase over the three-year period would be 19.10% and not 18% (6% + 6% + 6%).

This process of multiplying works in the same manner for price increases. For example, if the cost of a $10,000 automobile increased at a rate of 6% per year (the automobile's inflation rate), at the end of a three-year period, the item would cost $11,910.

Both of these examples illustrate the compounding process because we are:

(1) Multiplying; and

(2) Applying the annual rate of increase to the previous year's *entire* ending amount.

These two rules set the compounding process in motion.

Table 1.1 shows what happens when $10,000 is invested for a twelve-year period at a 6% annual after-tax rate of return.

Table 1.1 *Mutual Fund Investment*

Year	Mutual Fund Investment	Annual Rate of Increase
	$10,000 × 1.06 =	
1	10,600.00	6%
2	11,236.00	6
3	11,910.16	6
4	12,624.77	6
5	13,382.26	6
6	14,185.20	6
7	15,036.31	6
8	15,938.49	6
9	16,894.80	6
10	17,908.49	6
11	18,983.00	6
12	20,121.98	6
	100%	72%

As you examine Table 1.1, you'll note three points:

(1) The annual rate of increase is 6% per year–a total of 72% for the twelve-year period.

(2) Each year's annual rate of return is not added to the growing investment amount; rather, it is multiplied–that is, each prior year's ending amount is multiplied by 1.06 to arrive at the current year's amount. This sets the compounding process in motion.

(3) Although the annual rates of return (which are 6% in our example) total 72, there has actually been a 100% increase in the original investment amount. Thus, the original $10,000 has increased to $20,000 (actually $20,121.98).

Living Costs

Just as the compounding process works with all types of investment returns, it also affects the cost of all the items you purchase for day-to-day living. This includes the cost of food, a car, a home, and a college education.

The compounding process is at work increasing the cost of the goods and services you buy because the annual percentage increase that occurs in an item's cost is applied against the previous year's entire ending amount–using multiplication. Let's consider our earlier example of an automobile that costs $10,000. If that automobile increases in price at 6% per year, its cost will rise to $10,600 at the end of year 1 ($10,000 x 1.06). If the increases continue at 6% for a total of twelve years, at the end of year 12 the cost of the automobile will increase (double) to approximately $20,000–a 100% increase. Table 1.2 illustrates this phenomenon.

Table 1.2 *Automobile Price Increase*

Year	Price of Automobile	Annual Rate of Increase
	$10,000 × 1.06 =	
1	10,600.00	6%
2	11,236.00	6
3	11,910.16	6
4	12,624.77	6
5	13,382.26	6
6	14,185.20	6
7	15,036.31	6
8	15,938.49	6
9	16,894.80	6
10	17,908.49	6
11	18,983.00	6
12	20,121.98	6
	100%	**72%**

When examining Table 1.2, remember that the compounding process is in effect. This means that the percentage rate of increase, 6%, is applied to each year's entire ending amount (not the original beginning amount). In this example, the 6% annual rate of increase is applied against each previous year's amount (multiplying by 1.06) to arrive at the current year's amount. During the twelve-year period, the annual percentage increases total 72; however, the annual cost of the automobile increases from $10,000 to $20,121.98 (slightly more than $20,000)–again a 100% increase.

In summary, the compounding process works by using each year's entire ending amount and the laws of multiplication. In our example, each year's ending amount is multiplied by 1.06 to arrive at the following year's amount.

The Number 72

The number 72 is an extremely important number. It enables you to quickly estimate the length of time it takes money to double when invested at a uniform annual compound rate of return. A uniform rate of return means the rate of return is the same year in and year out; it is fixed (constant). The number 72 will also enable you to estimate the length of time it will take for your living costs to double based on inflation. Let's begin by examining investment return.

Suppose you earn a 6% uniform annual after-tax rate of return on an investment. Divide 72 by 6 and you get 12. That is the number of years it will take your money, invested at a 6% uniform annual after-tax rate of return, to double while the compounding process is in operation.

Table 1.3 *Rule of 72 Equations*

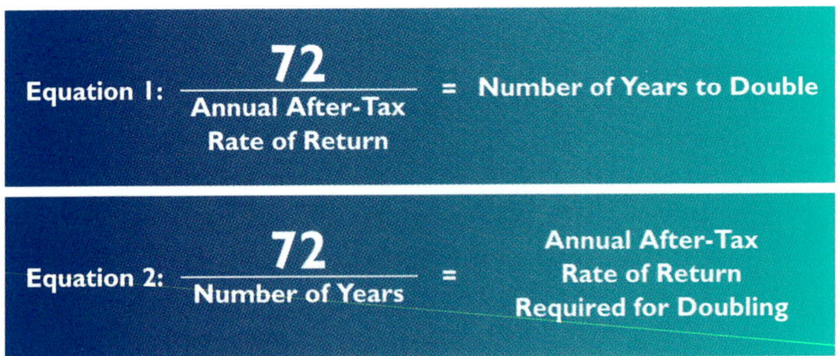

It will be helpful if you memorize the two equations in Table 1.3 as we will be using them frequently throughout this financial planning system. The first equation divides the number 72 by the annual after-tax rate of return on an investment to arrive at the number of years it will take for an original invested amount to double. The second equation divides the number 72 by the number of years to determine the annual after-tax rate of return required on your investment for the original invested amount to double. Note that in addition to the annual investment return rate being uniform (constant), the compounding process must be in operation for the number 72 to be used in either equation.

Table 1.4 illustrates the use of both formulas. As you examine the annual after-tax rates of return in this table, keep in mind that the rule of 72 works with the after-tax returns on *any* type of investment. This includes savings accounts, money market accounts, certificates of deposit, and all types of mutual funds. It also works with increases in living costs due to inflation.

Table 1.4 *Doubling at Various After-Tax Rates of Return*

Annual Rate of Return	Number of Years
4%	18.00
5	14.40
6	12.00
7	10.30
8	9.00
9	8.00
10	7.20
11	6.60
12	6.00

Table 1.4 indicates the number of years required to double an original amount invested at various annual after-tax rates of return. (The table also shows the annual after-tax rate of return you would need to earn in order to double your original investment amount in a specified number of years.) From the table, you can quickly observe that at a 6% annual after-tax rate of return, your money doubles in twelve years; at a 9% annual after-tax rate of return, it doubles in eight years; and at a 12% rate, it doubles in six years. Remember that the uniform (constant) rates of return in this table would not produce a doubling during the stated number of years if the compounding process were not in effect.

The point is this: The number 72 works with annual percentage changes, whether they are the annual percentage changes of an investment or the annual percentage change in the cost of an item. This is because the rule of 72 is based on both the mathematical laws of multiplication and the compounding process, which in turn is based on cumulative reinvestment (applying the increase to the prior year's entire ending amount).

Up until now, we have discussed using the rule of 72 only when the annual percentage changes are uniform (that is, constant from year to year). Now, however, we will take the rule of 72 one step further and analyze its accuracy when the annual percentage changes vary (that is, they are not uniform from year to year). To do this, let's look at two investment scenarios. In each, there will be a $100 investment and a twelve-year period.

In the first scenario, the annual percentage returns will be positive and they will be single-digit returns; however, the rates will vary (be nonuniform). In the second scenario, the annual percentage returns will be both positive and negative and single- and double-digit. What we are trying to determine is whether the number 72 is still accurate for determining a doubling even when the annual percentage rates are nonuniform, negative, or double-digit numbers.

Table 1.5 *The Rule of 72 for Nonuniform Returns*

Positive Single-Digit Rates of Return			Positive and Negative Single- and Double-Digit Rates of Return		
Year	**Annual Rate of Return**	**Cumulative Investment Balance**	**Year**	**Annual Rate of Return**	**Cumulative Investment Balance**
		$100.00			$100.00
1	**8%**	108.00	1	**4%**	104.00
2	**9**	117.72	2	**13**	117.52
3	**5**	123.61	3	**17**	137.50
4	**3**	127.32	4	**6**	145.75
5	**7**	136.23	5	**-8**	134.09
6	**8**	147.13	6	**-10**	120.68
7	**4**	153.02	7	**16**	139.99
8	**1**	154.55	8	**18**	165.19
9	**6**	163.82	9	**-10**	148.67
10	**6**	173.65	10	**-6**	139.75
11	**8**	187.54	11	**12**	156.52
12	**7**	200.67	12	**20**	187.82
Total	**72%**		**Total**	**72%**	

As Table 1.5 shows, when an initial $100 investment increases by annual rates of return that are positive single-digit, and nonuniform (refer to the left-hand side of the table), the initial $100 grows to $200.67–a 100.67% increase–when the annual rates of return total 72. When the $100 investment increases by annual rates of return that are positive and negative and single- and double-digit (refer to the right-hand side of the table), the initial $100 investment grows to only $187.82–an 87.82% increase–when the annual rates of return total 72. Although the accuracy of the rule of 72 is diminished somewhat by negative and double-digit rates of return, the rule remains a good estimate for *positive,* nonuniform annual rates of return (positive returns that vary from year to year). In this financial planning system, we will be applying the rule of 72 primarily to inflation rates–measuring the increases in the cost of goods and services–that have been, for the most part, positive and nonuniform since 1949. This will allow us to determine when a doubling occurs in the item under analysis.

For example, if we apply the rule of 72 to annual inflation rates as measured by the Consumer Price Index (which measures change in the average price level for goods and services), when we attain the number 72, the average price for goods and services will have doubled. See Module 3 for more information about the CPI. Similarly, if we use the rule of 72 in adding inflation rates for new home prices or college costs, (rates which differ from the inflation rates for goods and services), when we reach the number 72, the cost of a new home or a college education will have doubled.

Recap: You have now reached an important milestone. You have learned that the rule of 72 gives a quick *estimate* of when an original amount will double. The number 72 can be used with the annual after-tax rates of return for any type of investment or for the annual percentage changes in the cost of any item.

Keep in mind that you arrive at the number 72 by *adding* together annual rates. Those rates, however, are actually being applied by multiplication to each prior year's *entire* ending balance (*not* just the initial amount), to arrive at the current year's ending balance. That is why you actually reach a 100% increase when the individual annual rates only add up to 72.

An interesting analogy can be made with the fable "The Tortoise and the Hare." In this fable, there is a race between a slow-moving (uniform) tortoise and a fast-moving (nonuniform) hare. As it turns out, the hare loses the race even though he can run at a faster pace than the tortoise. This is because his pace was irregular–that is, he would stop and start, similar to negative and positive rates of return on an investment. It is important to understand that steady rates of return can sometimes produce better results over the long run than irregular, nonuniform returns. (We will return to this concept later in the book.)

Calculating Annual and Total Return

Two formulas are used to measure the percentage investment return from year to year or from the beginning of an investment period to the end of an investment period. They are the annual rate of return formula and the total rate of return formula. These formulas can be used to calculate not only the return on an investment, but also the annual percentage change and the total percentage change. These formulas are used throughout the book, so it is important that you understand these concepts. For example, in Module 2, we will show you how the formulas apply to increases in living costs.

We will now use these two formulas to calculate the annual rate of return and the total return in the positive, single-digit rate of return on investment scenario shown previously in Table 1.5. Our calculation of the annual rate of return will be for the end of year 2, and our calculation of the total rate of return will be for the end of year 12. At the end of year 2, the investment amount is $117.72, and the annual rate of return is 9.00%. At the end of year 12, the investment amount is $200.67, and the total rate of return is 100.67%. Note that in Table 1.5, *each year's ending balance becomes the next year's beginning balance* when using these formulas.

Annual Rate of Return

Whether the ending investment amount is increasing or decreasing from year to year, the equation for calculating the annual rate of return is as follows:

$$\text{Annual Rate of Return} = \left[\frac{\text{End of Year Balance} - \text{Beginning of Year Balance}}{\text{Beginning of Year Balance}}\right] \times 100$$

$$= \frac{117.72 - 108}{108} \times 100$$

$$= 9.00\%$$

Total Rate of Return

Similarly, whether the ending cumulative investment balance is increasing or decreasing from year to year, the equation for calculating the total rate of return is as shown below. Note that in this formula the denominator of the equation is now the *original* investment amount, whereas in the previous formula, it was the beginning-of-year balance:

$$\text{Total Rate of Return} = \left[\frac{\text{Ending Year Balance} - \text{Original Investment Amount}}{\text{Original Investment Amount}}\right] \times 100$$

$$= \frac{200.67 - 100}{100} \times 100$$

$$= 100.67\%$$

Future Doublings

So far in Module 1 we have discussed how the rule of 72 can be used to determine when an investment will double (or any item under analysis, for that matter). We'll now explain what happens at the second, third, and fourth doublings – regardless of whether these doublings occur quickly because of large annual percentage changes or slowly because of small annual percentage changes.

Here is an example: If $100 is invested and increases to $200, the original $100 investment amount has doubled – that is, it is equal to two times the original investment amount. This doubling will occur when the annual percentage changes (rates of return) total 72.

If the $200 investment amount remains invested and doubles again–the second doubling– the ending investment amount will increase from $200 to $400. This amount will then be equal to four times the original $100 investment and will occur when the annual percentage changes again total 72.

If the $400 remains invested and doubles again – the third doubling – the ending investment amount will increase to $800, which is equal to eight times the original investment. This third doubling will occur when the annual percentage changes total 72 once more.

If the $800 remains invested and doubles yet again – the fourth doubling – the ending investment amount will increase from $800 to $1,600. The ending $1,600 investment will now equal sixteen times the original $100, and it will occur when the annual percentage changes again total 72.

These increases at the time of each doubling–from $100 to $200, $200 to $400, $400 to $800, and $800 to $1,600–are due to the *compounding process.* Thus, if a $100 investment increases at an annual rate of 6% for forty-eight years (totaling 72 four times), the $100 investment would double four times to $1,600. These doublings are illustrated in Table 1.6 and will be referred to throughout later modules, so you may wish to refer back to this table.

Table 1.6 *Future Doublings*

A	B	C	D
Total of Percentage Rates	**Number of Doublings**	**Dollar Amount**	**Total Percentage Change**
		$100	
72	1	200	100%
72	2	400	300
72	3	800	700
72	4	1,600	1,500

The power of the compounding process is evident in the percentage changes (column D) at each doubling. Note that at the first doubling, the total percentage change is 100%; at the second doubling, it is 300%; at the third, 700%; and at the fourth doubling, 1,500%.

The reason that the size of the percentage increases begins to snowball at the second, third, and fourth doublings is because the compounding process works by using *each year's entire ending amount.* As a result, the annual 6% rate of increase is applied against an increasing amount. Note that when you add the percentage rates in column A, they total 288% (72% x 4). However, the total percentage increase at the fourth doubling is 1,500% (column D). This additional 1,212% increase (from 288% to 1,500%) is the result of the compounding process.

Module 2 Compounding Inflation

Welcome to Module 2, "Compounding Inflation." In this module, we will link the compounding process to the economic concept of inflation. To gain a proper perspective on the history of inflation in the United States, we must first select a base year (a starting point against which we will measure change). For our purposes, the base year will be 1949. Let us explain why we chose 1949.

When examining historical economic data and the investment performance of past financial markets, it is standard in the financial planning industry to start with information dating as far back as 1926. This approach, however, incorporates time periods that are atypical (where events differ significantly from the usual ebb and flow of economic activity).

For example, in 1929 our country experienced the great stock market crash, followed by the Great Depression that lasted throughout the 1930s. This set the stage for a bear (weak) market for common stocks (where stock prices are generally declining or static), which started with the 1929 crash and continued through 1949 (a period of twenty-one years). Further, as a result of the stock market crash and the Depression, the 1930s were a deflationary period, where the price level for goods and services was generally falling.

Then World War II began in 1941 and lasted into 1945. Not only was this a war period, but it was also a period of high inflation. The next three years (1946 through 1948) were a time when pent-up consumer demand, that had accumulated during the war years, was unleashed in the form of increased spending (also a period of high inflation). Overall, the eight years from 1941 through 1948 were marked by high inflation due to increased government spending to finance the war effort (1941–1945) and increased consumer spending during the years immediately following (1946–1948).

There is another reason we have chosen 1949 as our beginning point of reference for measuring inflation. Except for the eight-year period from 1941 through 1948, ongoing inflation in the United States was almost nonexistent prior to 1949, even as far back as the late 1700s. Furthermore, inflation was primarily associated with periods of war. It was only *after 1949* that inflation became both prevalent and continuous in the United States.

For these reasons, we have chosen 1949 as the starting point—our benchmark year—from which to study inflation. This will allow us to examine economic data and trends from time periods that are more likely to resemble what may occur in the future.

Calculating Compounding Inflation

Inflation is defined as *a rise in the average price level of consumer goods and services*. Deflation, on the other hand, is defined as *a decline in the average price level of consumer goods and services*. As a standard rule, when prices rise, living costs increase; when prices fall, living costs decrease. It is rising prices (inflation) that are our main concern.

In Module 1, the number 72 was used to calculate how many years it would take an investment to double at an annual compound uniform (constant) or nonuniform (fluctuating) after-tax rate of return. Inflation is a rate which is also subject to compounding, so in Module 2, we will apply the number 72 to annual rates of inflation to demonstrate how the concept affects the cost side of your personal finances.

In planning for a secure financial future, wouldn't you find it useful to be able to estimate how inflation is likely to affect the amount of money you will need in the future to maintain (or improve) your current standard of living? The rule of 72 can help you do that because annual rates of inflation compound in exactly the same way as annual after-tax rates of return on an investment. To illustrate the mechanics of how a doubling occurs in living costs, let's look at an example.

To calculate the increase or decrease in living costs over time, annual inflation (or deflation) rates must first be changed into conversion factors. Using the conversion formula, conversion factors are calculated by dividing annual rates of inflation (or deflation) by 100 and then adding the whole number 1, as in this equation:

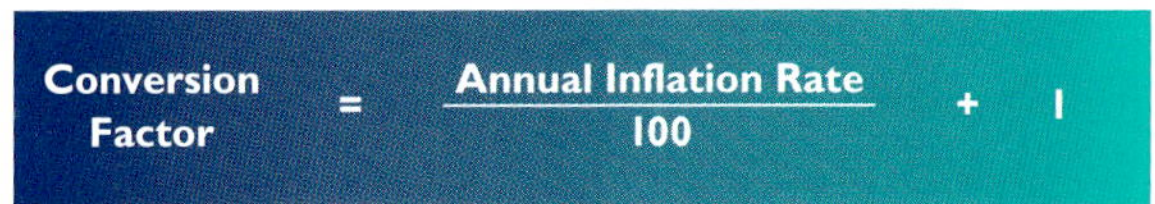

$$\text{Conversion Factor} = \frac{\text{Annual Inflation Rate}}{100} + 1$$

For example, if the annual inflation rate is 6%, dividing 6 by 100 equals .06, and adding 1 equals 1.06. The 6% inflation rate is now a conversion factor of 1.06. The process of converting annual rates of inflation or deflation into conversion factors is necessary to calculate the effect of compounding inflation or deflation.

Using the conversion formula, we can now calculate the total increase in living costs during a twelve-year period when the annual rate of inflation is 6% per year. (Note, however, that inflation rates are typically not constant from year to year, but vary. We are using an annual 6% inflation rate for twelve years in this example to show a doubling in living costs with *the rule of 72)*.

Table 2.1 *Calculating Compounding Inflation*

A	B	C	D
Year	**Inflation Rate**	**Conversion Factor**	**Index Value**
			100.00
1	6	1.06	**106.00**
2	6	1.06	**112.36**
3	6	1.06	**119.10**
4	6	1.06	**126.25**
5	6	1.06	**133.83**
6	6	1.06	**141.86**
7	6	1.06	**150.37**
8	6	1.06	**159.39**
9	6	1.06	**168.95**
10	6	1.06	**179.09**
11	6	1.06	**189.84**
12	6	1.06	**201.23**

Table 2.1 illustrates the mechanics of compounding inflation. When measuring the change in the price level over time, it is standard to begin with a base index value of 100.00 (column D). The index will then increase or decrease annually, depending on whether price changes are inflationary or deflationary. In year 1, the 6% inflation rate (column B) is converted to a conversion factor of 1.06 (column C) using the conversion formula just presented. The index value, which begins with 100, is then multiplied by the conversion factor in year 1, which yields 106.00. The index value of 106.00 for year 1 is then increased by the conversion factor for year 2 to yield 112.36.

It is important to realize that the process of multiplying the entire index value each year by the next year's conversion factor results in the compound increase (or decrease) in the index value. The total percentage change for the two-year period (years 1 and 2) is 12.36% (column D). This is slightly more than the sum of the inflation rates for years 1 and 2, which is 12% (column B). Thus, the compounding process has already begun in year 2.

Over the twelve-year period, the price level for goods and services—which is what the values shown in column D really convey—increases to 201.23. Although the annual rates of inflation total only 72, the total percentage increase is 101.23%. This increase is calculated by applying the equation introduced in Module 1 for determining the total rate of return to the index values in column D. (The annual percentage changes from year to year – the 6% inflation rates shown in column B – can be calculated by applying the annual rate of return equation in Module 1 to the index values in column D.) When using either equation, keep in mind that we are now working with beginning and ending year index values (as opposed to investment amounts) to determine the annual and total percentage changes.

Let's take a closer look at inflation in the United States from 1949 through 1994, as measured by the Consumer Price Index of urban consumers (CPI-U). To do this, we'll divide this forty-six-year period into three time segments as follows:

(1) The twenty-year period from 1949 through 1968 (Table 2.2);
(2) The thirteen-year period from 1969 through 1981 (Table 2.3); and
(3) The thirteen-year period from 1982 to 1994 (Table 2.4).

(The full time period, 1949–1994, will be used in our study of financial market performance in a subsequent module.)

In addition to a brief review of each of these three time segments, we'll also combine the three segments to show the total increase in living costs from 1949–1994 (Table 2.5). The increases in each of these tables were calculated using the mechanics of calculating compounding inflation shown in Table 2.1, along with the actual rates of inflation (deflation) for those time periods. (Although our beginning year for analyzing inflation is 1949, the CPI provides information as far back as 1913 should you ever have a need for it.)

Table 2.2 *Inflation Rates: 1949-1968*

Year	Percent	Year	Percent
1949	-2.10%	1960	1.40%
1950	5.90	1961	0.70
1951	6.00	1962	1.30
1952	0.80	1963	1.60
1953	0.70	1964	1.00
1954	-0.70	1965	1.90
1955	0.40	1966	3.50
1956	3.00	1967	3.00
1957	2.90	1968	4.70
1958	1.80	1949–68	47.00%
1959	1.70		

Source: U.S. Department of Labor, Bureau of Labor Statistics.

The first segment, the twenty-year period from 1949 through 1968, is presented in Table 2.2. The total inflation for this period was 47%. The average annual rate of inflation was 1.96%. (Note that the average is not calculated by adding the inflation rates and then dividing by the number of years, but by taking the annualized rate which is a geometric average based on multiplication). This only makes sense since the increase in living costs does not increase arithmetically; rather, it increases by multiplication using the conversion formula. The twenty-year period, 1949 through 1968, was a period of low inflation.

Table 2.3 *Inflation Rates: 1969–1981*

Year	Percent	Year	Percent
1969	6.20%	1976	4.90%
1970	5.60	1977	6.70
1971	3.30	1978	9.00
1972	3.40	1979	13.30
1973	8.70	1980	12.50
1974	12.30	1981	8.90
1975	6.90	1969–81	165.00%

Source: U.S. Department of Labor, Bureau of Labor Statistics.

The second segment, the thirteen-year period from 1969 through 1981, is presented in Table 2.3. During this period, a serious problem arose: Inflation increased to an average annual rate of 7.78%–a dramatic increase compared to the average 1.96% annual rate during the previous twenty years. The total inflation increase for the thirteen years from 1969 through 1981 was 165%. This was clearly a period of high inflation.

Table 2.4 *Inflation Rates: 1982–1994*

Year	Percent	Year	Percent
1982	3.80%	1989	4.60%
1983	3.80	1990	6.10
1984	3.90	1991	3.10
1985	3.80	1992	2.90
1986	1.10	1993	2.70
1987	4.40	1994	2.70
1988	4.40	1982–94	59.00%

Source: U.S. Department of Labor, Bureau of Labor Statistics.

The third segment, the thirteen-year period from 1982 through 1994, is presented in Table 2.4. The total increase in inflation for this period was 59%, and the average annual rate of inflation was 3.63%. During this period, inflation was moderate.

Table 2.5 shows the total increase in living costs during the forty-six-year period from 1949 through 1994. As you study this table, you'll note that it works in exactly the same manner as Table 2.1, "Calculating Compounding Inflation." The only difference is that columns E and F have been added. Column E, "Sum of Inflation Rates," is a running total of the annual inflation rates, and column F, "Approximate Time of Doubling," indicates the approximate time when each doubling in living costs occurred.

As you examine Table 2.5, keep in mind that we are measuring increases in living costs by using a beginning index value (price level) of 100, which can be thought of as 100 cents or $1.00. Also note that the compounding process is in operation–that is, each year's inflation rate is first changed to a conversion factor. It is then applied to each previous year's entire index value (by multiplying) to arrive at the current year's index value. As you will see, the increases at each doubling will occur in exactly the same way they would if they were applied to an original $100 investment.

Table 2.5 *Compounding Inflation during 1949-1994*

A	B	C	D	E	F
Year	Inflation Rate	Conversion Factor	Index Value	Sum of Inflation Rates	Approximate Time of Doubling
			100.00		
1949	-2.10	.979	97.90	-2.10	
1950	5.90	1.059	103.68	3.80	
1951	6.00	1.06	109.90	9.80	
1952	0.80	1.008	110.78	10.60	
1953	0.70	1.007	111.56	11.30	
1954	-0.70	.993	110.78	10.60	
1955	0.40	1.004	111.22	11.00	
1956	3.00	1.03	114.56	14.00	
1957	2.90	1.029	117.88	16.90	
1958	1.80	1.018	120.00	18.70	
1959	1.70	1.017	122.04	20.40	
1960	1.40	1.014	123.75	21.80	
1961	0.70	1.007	124.62	22.50	
1962	1.30	1.013	126.24	23.80	
1963	1.60	1.016	128.26	25.40	
1964	1.00	1.01	129.54	26.40	
1965	1.90	1.019	132.00	28.30	
1966	3.50	1.035	136.62	31.80	
1967	3.00	1.03	140.72	34.80	
1968	4.70	1.047	147.33	39.50	
1969	6.20	1.062	156.46	45.70	
1970	5.60	1.056	165.22	51.30	
1971	3.30	1.033	170.67	54.60	
1972	3.40	1.034	176.47	58.00	
1973	8.70	1.087	191.82	66.70	
1974	**5.30**	**1.053**	**201.99**	**72.00**	**First Doubling**
1975	13.90	1.139	230.07	13.90	
1976	4.90	1.049	241.34	18.80	
1977	6.70	1.067	257.51	25.50	
1978	9.00	1.09	280.69	34.50	
1979	13.30	1.133	318.02	47.80	
1980	12.50	1.125	357.77	60.30	
1981	8.90	1.089	389.61	69.20	
1982	**2.80**	**1.028**	**400.52**	**72.00**	**Second Doubling**
1983	4.80	1.048	419.74	4.80	
1984	3.90	1.039	436.11	8.70	
1985	3.80	1.038	452.68	12.50	
1986	1.10	1.011	457.66	13.60	
1987	4.40	1.044	477.80	18.00	
1988	4.40	1.044	498.82	22.40	
1989	4.60	1.046	521.77	27.00	
1990	6.10	1.061	553.60	33.10	
1991	3.10	1.031	570.76	36.20	
1992	2.90	1.029	587.31	39.10	
1993	2.70	1.027	603.17	41.80	
1994	2.70	1.027	619.46	44.50	

Source: U.S. Department of Labor, Bureau of Labor Statistics. Note that the annual inflation rates for 1974 and 1982 were actually 12.30% and 3.80%. However, only the amounts necessary to reach a total of 72 (column E) were included for those years. The excess amounts were placed into the following years.

Notice that each time the annual rates of inflation total 72 in column E of Table 2.5, a doubling occurs in the price level in column D. (Actually, it exceeds an exact doubling.) Doublings are occurring, despite the nonuniform and negative (1949 and 1954) annual rates of inflation. At the end of 1994, the price level had increased from 100 to over 619. This represents an increase of 519%.

Therefore, goods and services that cost $1.00 at the beginning of 1949 increased to $6.19 by the end of 1994. The average rate of inflation for the forty-six-year period was 4.04%, or 4% rounded to the nearest whole number.

Now you are beginning to get a glimpse of how the prices of goods and services escalated so rapidly since 1949. This escalation is more than the result of simple arithmetic; it is due to *compounding inflation*. We will now explore the concept of compounding inflation in more detail.

Examining Compounding Inflation

Two doublings have occurred in living costs during the forty-six-year period covered by Table 2.5. The first doubling occurred in 1974; the second in 1982.

During the twenty-six years from 1949 through 1974, the annual rates of inflation varied from a low of -2.10% in 1949 to a high of 12.30% in 1974. Because the annual rates of inflation remained low, it took twenty-six years for the rates to total 72. These low rates of inflation slowed the compounding process. This, in turn, lengthened the time period for the first doubling to take place.

The second doubling occurred at the end of 1982. That's because annual rates of inflation were much higher during this eight-year period (1975 through 1982) than they were during the previous twenty-six years (1949 through 1974).

At the time of the first doubling in 1974, the ending index value (column D), which represents the price level, increased to 201.99. At the time of the second doubling in 1982, the ending index value increased to 400.52. When we reach the third doubling (probably in the year 2004 if we continue at a constant 2.7% rate of inflation), living costs will have increased to an index value of 800—representing a 700% increase over the base year of 1949.

Keep in mind that the price level is increasing at a compound rate, doubling every time the annual rates of inflation total 72, because each year's inflation rate, as a conversion factor, is being applied to the prior year's entire index value in column D. This index value is analogous to the return on investment we discussed in Module 1 where the annual rate of return is applied to the prior year's cumulative investment amount to obtain the current year's cumulative investment amount.

On the date of the third doubling, the annual rates of inflation will have totaled 72 three times. Although multiplying 72 by 3 equals only 216%, the total increase in inflation will be 700%. The compounding process accounts for the remaining 484%.

Table 2.6 illustrates the increase in the price level at the time of each doubling. Note that this table also appeared in Module 1. The only differences are that: (1) instead of measuring the total percentage change to an original $100 investment, we are now measuring the total percentage change in the price level from a beginning index of 100; and (2) the price level increases by the annual rates of inflation rather than by investment return.

Table 2.6 *Future Doublings*

A	B	C	D
Total of Inflation Rates	**Number of Doublings**	**Index Value**	**Total Percentage Change**
		100	
72	**1**	200	100%
72	**2**	400	300
72	**3**	800	700
72	**4**	1,600	1,500

Table 2.6 indicates the total percentage change (column D) at the time of each doubling. Remember that when the annual rates of inflation total 72, the price level doubles (column C). At the third doubling—which has not yet occurred—an item that cost $1.00 in 1949 will cost $8.00.

If we use 1949 as the base year for comparison, we are approaching the third doubling in living costs in the United States. *Did you catch that?* Using the number 72 and adding the annual rates of inflation, the first doubling took place in 1974, the second in 1982, and the third is on its way.

Now we'll apply the rule of 72 to inflation rates for home costs, college costs, and retirement costs.

Table 2.7 *New Home Costs*

A	B	C	D	E
Year	Annual Inflation	Sum of Rates	Annual Cost	Approximate Time of Doubling
1963			$ 18,000	
1964	5.00%	5.00%	$ 18,900	
1965	5.82%	10.82%	$ 20,000	
1966	7.00%	17.82%	$ 21,400	
1967	6.08%	23.90%	$ 22,700	
1968	8.81%	32.71%	$ 24,700	
1969	3.65%	36.35%	$ 25,600	
1970	-8.60%	27.76%	$ 23,400	
1971	7.69%	35.45%	$ 25,200	
1972	9.52%	44.97%	$ 27,600	
1973	17.75%	62.72%	$ 32,500	
1974	9.28%	**72.00%**	**$ 35,500**	**Approximate First Doubling**
1975	10.66%	10.66%	$ 39,300	
1976	12.47%	23.12%	$ 44,200	
1977	10.41%	33.53%	$ 48,800	
1978	14.14%	47.67%	$ 55,700	
1979	12.93%	60.60%	$ 62,900	
1980	2.70%	63.30%	$ 64,600	
1981	6.66%	69.96%	$ 68,900	
1982	0.58%	70.54%	$ 69,300	
1983	1.46%	**72.00%**	**$ 70,300**	**Approximate Second Doubling**
1984	13.64%	13.64%	$ 79,900	
1985	5.51%	19.14%	$ 84,300	
1986	9.13%	28.28%	$ 92,000	
1987	13.59%	41.86%	$104,500	
1988	7.66%	49.52%	$112,500	
1989	6.67%	56.19%	$120,000	
1990	2.42%	58.60%	$122,900	
1991	-2.36%	56.24%	$120,000	
1992	1.25%	57.49%	$121,500	
1993	4.12%	61.61%	$126,500	
1994	2.77%	64.38%	$130,000	

Source: U.S. Department of Housing and Urban Development. Note that the annual inflation rates for 1974 and 1983 were actually 10.46% and 8.66%. However, only the amounts necessary to reach a total of 72 (column C) were included for those years. The excess amounts were placed into the following years.

New Home Costs

Column B of Table 2.7 lists the annual inflation rates for new homes during the period 1963–1994. (The government did not begin compiling data until 1963.) We are using costs for new homes (as opposed to existing homes) because the data for new homes are adjusted to hold the quality of a home constant so that only price changes are reflected from year to year, rather than price increases that could be attributed to upgrading the home.

The annual inflation rates in column B are totaled in column C. By applying the rule of 72, we see that the first doubling in new home costs occurred in 1974 and the second in 1983. The numbers in column D are calculated by applying each year's inflation rate (column B) to the prior year's annual cost (column D) using the conversion formula.

At the time of the first doubling, the cost of a home increased from $18,000 in 1963 to $35,500 in 1974–almost a complete doubling. (The deflation rate of -8.60% in 1970 slowed the compounding process and diminished the accuracy of the number 72 for calculating an exact doubling). At the second doubling, the cost of a home increased from $35,500 in 1974 to $70,300 in 1983–again, almost a complete doubling. (Keep in mind that the rule of 72 only *estimates* the time of a doubling).

At the time of the third doubling, the cost of a new home will increase to approximately $144,000–which is 700% more than the $18,000 cost in 1963. If the compounding process were not in operation, the price of a new home would have increased to only $56,880 representing a 216% increase (72 x 3 = 216%).

One final point about housing inflation: Annual inflation rates for new homes differ from inflation affecting living costs. This is primarily a result of different demand and supply considerations for housing as opposed to that for general goods and services. This can lead to housing costs increasing at a greater (or lesser) rate than general living costs–an important concept to note when projecting future costs.

Now let's examine private college costs.

College Costs

Table 2.8 presents the average annual cost of a private college education (Column D), starting with the 1964-1965 school year and ending with the 1993–1994 school year. These costs include tuition, room, and board. (Keep in mind that a typical college year begins in the fall and ends in the spring. As a result, the annual cost of a college education covers parts of two different years, which is reflected in the table.)

The annual inflation rates for a private college education during the 1964–1994 period are shown in column B (data are not available any earlier than 1964). The annual inflation rates in column B are totaled in column C. The numbers in column D are calculated by applying each year's inflation rate (column B) to the prior year's annual cost (column D) using the conversion formula.

The first doubling occurred during school year 1976–1977 (when the annual inflation rates totaled 72), the second doubling occurred during school year 1984–1985, and the third doubling occurred during school year 1993–1994. At the first doubling, the cost of a private college education increased from $1,907 in 1964–1965 to $3,831 (a complete doubling). At the second doubling, the annual cost of a private college education increased from $3,831 in 1976–1977 to $7,604 in 1984–1985 (almost a complete doubling). The annual cost at the third doubling increased from $7,604 in 1984–1985 to $15,132 in 1993–1994 (almost a complete doubling).

The $15,132 figure is nearly 700% more than the $1,907 cost in 1964–1965. Note that if the compounding process were not in operation, the price of a one-year private college education would have increased to only $6,026 representing a 216% increase (72 x 3 = 216%) during the period 1964–1994. As with housing inflation, college inflation differs from inflation affecting living costs. This is primarily a result of different demand and supply considerations for college costs as opposed to that for general goods and services. This can lead to college costs increasing at a greater (or lesser) rate than general living costs. As with inflation affecting housing costs, this is an important concept to keep in mind when projecting your future costs.

Finally, let's examine retirement costs.

Retirement Costs

When preparing projections for retirement, you should base the inflation rate on expected increases in living costs. As we mentioned earlier, the average annual rate of inflation for the years 1949–1994 was 4%. This is a good long-term, average rate of inflation for use in projecting future living costs. At a 4% annual rate of inflation, living costs will double every eighteen years. What this means is that to maintain the same standard of living currently provided by $40,000, one will need $80,000 in eighteen years.

Table 2.8 *Private College Costs*

A	B	C	D	E
Year	Annual Inflation	Sum of Rates	Annual Cost	Approximate Time of Doubling
1964–1965			$ 1,907	
1965–1966	5.14%	5.14%	$ 2,005	
1966–1967	5.94%	11.08%	$ 2,124	
1967–1968	3.81%	14.89%	$ 2,205	
1968–1969	5.26%	20.15%	$ 2,321	
1969–1970	9.00%	29.15%	$ 2,530	
1970–1971	8.22%	37.37%	$ 2,738	
1971–1972	6.54%	43.91%	$ 2,917	
1972–1973	4.15%	48.06%	$ 3,038	
1973–1974	4.15%	52.21%	$ 3,164	
1974–1975	7.55%	59.76%	$ 3,403	
1975–1976	7.64%	67.40%	$ 3,663	
1976–1977	4.60%	**72.00%**	**$ 3,831**	First Doubling
1977–1978	8.53%	8.53%	$ 4,158	
1978–1979	8.56%	17.09%	$ 4,514	
1979–1980	8.82%	25.91%	$ 4,912	
1980–1981	11.36%	37.27%	$ 5,470	
1981–1982	12.72%	49.99%	$ 6,166	
1982–1983	12.23%	62.22%	$ 6,920	
1983–1984	8.50%	70.72%	$ 7,508	
1984–1985	1.28%	**72.00%**	**$ 7,604**	Second Doubling
1985–1986	16.84%	16.84%	$ 8,885	
1986–1987	8.90%	25.74%	$ 9,676	
1987–1988	8.64%	34.38%	$ 10,512	
1988–1989	6.44%	40.82%	$ 11,189	
1989–1990	7.41%	48.23%	$ 12,018	
1990–1991	7.42%	55.65%	$ 12,910	
1991–1992	7.72%	63.37%	$ 13,907	
1992–1993	5.23%	68.60%	$ 14,634	
1993–1994	3.40%	**72.00%**	**$15,132**	Third Doubling

Source: U.S. Department of Education. Note that the annual inflation rates for 1976–1977, 1984–1985, and 1993–1994 were actually 6.63%, 9.24% and 6.14%. However, only the amounts necessary to reach a total of 72 (column C) were used for those years. The excess amounts were placed into the following years (except for 1993–1994 since the table ends in that year).

Module 3 The Consumer Price Index (CPI)

In this module, we will define the Consumer Price Index (CPI) and explain its usage as a tool for measuring the effect of inflation on living costs. Before we move into our discussion of the CPI, however, it is necessary that you understand the structure of the five-step economic model we will be using (as illustrated in Table 3.1) and how it is representative of our economic system. Understanding these five steps will enable you to pinpoint where the CPI fits into the model and into your financial planning process.

Think of the five-step economic model as an aerial view of the financial planning process. It gives you the big picture—similar to looking out of a plane window at the ground below.

Table 3.1 *The Five-Step Economic Model*

In our economy, all of our personal income from all sources, except those categories specifically exempted, constitutes gross income (step 1). Then we pay income taxes (step 2). The funds which remain are our after-tax income (step 3) which is spent to support living costs (step 4). Any amount that remains represents savings (step 5), which can be placed in many different types of investments to meet future financial goals.

As you learned in Module 2, compounding inflation has caused a significant increase in living costs since 1949. It is living costs–the fourth step in the five-step economic model–that are monitored by the Consumer Price Index. Let's discuss what the term living costs really means and explain exactly how the Consumer Price Index defines and measures changes in living costs.

Consumer Price Index Defined

The Consumer Price Index, as defined by the U.S. Department of Labor, Bureau of Labor Statistics, is *"a measure of the average change over time in the prices paid by urban consumers for a fixed market basket of consumer goods and services from A to Z."* A simpler definition is *a measure of the average change in retail prices over time.*

The CPI operates on a very basic premise. It utilizes a *fixed quantity* of goods and services of a *fixed quality*–a fixed market basket–and then reprices this fixed market basket over time. It accomplishes this by comparing the most recent aggregate costs of the fixed market basket to beginning aggregate costs (comparing a current period to a beginning period).

The Bureau of Labor Statistics calculates the CPI monthly for two groups. The first group consists of urban wage earners and clerical workers (the CPI-W), and the second group consists of all urban consumers (the CPI-U). The CPI-W was introduced during the early 1900s for use in wage negotiations. The CPI-U was introduced in 1978.

We will be using the CPI-U to monitor inflation since it is much more representative of consumers' buying habits than the CPI-W. This is because the CPI-U takes into account *the buying patterns* of professional and salaried workers, part-time workers, the self-employed, the unemployed, retired persons, wage earners, and clerical workers. Let's identify the major product groups that the CPI monitors for price changes by referring to Table 3.2.

Table 3.2 *CPI Product Groups*

1	Food and Beverages
2	Housing
3	Apparel and Upkeep
4	Transportation
5	Medical Care
6	Entertainment
7	Other Goods and Services

Source: U.S. Department of Labor.

Table 3.2 lists the seven primary product groups from which consumers purchase items for day-to-day living. From within each group certain items are selected for price monitoring. These items comprise the *fixed market basket of goods and services.* To give you an in-depth understanding of the CPI, we will now examine the items in all seven product groups.

Breakdown of CPI Product Groups

As we discuss the items that are monitored monthly for price changes, it is important to keep in mind that we are analyzing the components of a price index. The only way that inflation can be measured is to monitor the change in the price of selected items over time. Therefore, the items monitored–and how often they are monitored–are important factors in calculating the CPI reading. Let's look at each product group more closely:

- **Food and Beverages**, the first product group, includes cereals and bakery products, meats, poultry, fish, eggs, dairy products, fruits, vegetables, sugars, sweets, fats, oils, alcoholic beverages, nonalcoholic beverages, prepared foods (canned and frozen), and food purchased away from home (meals and snacks).
- **Housing**, the second group, includes renters' costs, homeowners' costs, household insurance, maintenance and repair costs, fuels and other utilities, house furnishings, electronic equipment (video and audio products), major household appliances, housekeeping supplies (cleaning, lawn, and garden products), and housekeeping services.
- **Apparel and Upkeep**, the third product group, includes men's and boys' apparel, women's and girls' apparel, infants' and toddlers' apparel, footwear, and other apparel services.
- **Transportation**, the fourth product group, is broken down into public and private transportation. Public transportation includes fares for buses, taxis, and other modes of transportation. Private transportation includes new cars, new trucks, new motorcycles, used cars, gasoline, maintenance, repairs, private transportation services (automobile insurance, automobile finance charges, and automobile fees), and transportation commodities (automobile parts and equipment).
- **Medical Care,** the fifth group, consists of medical care commodities (prescription drugs, nonprescription drugs, and medical supplies), and medical care services (professional services including medical services, physicians' services, dental services, eye care, hospital-related services, and health insurance).
- **Entertainment**, the sixth product group, includes entertainment commodities (reading materials, newspapers, magazines, sporting goods, and toys), and entertainment services (club memberships and admissions to movies, theaters, concerts, operas, and sporting events).
- **Other Goods and Services**, the seventh and last product group, consists of tobacco and smoking products, personal care goods and appliances, personal care services, and personal and educational expenses. (Personal expenses include fees for legal services, personal financial services, and funeral expenses; educational expenses include tuition and other school fees.)

Now that you are familiar with the items in each product group (although we have not mentioned every item within each group), it should be evident that the CPI provides broad coverage of the major items that a consumer purchases. This leads us to two important points regarding the CPI.

First, the CPI, often referred to as a living cost index, is a statistical measure of the average change in prices of goods and services purchased by urban consumers for daily living. *While it measures price changes, it does not indicate how much a specific individual or family actually spends to live*. That is due to two factors. First, individual consumers and families sometimes change their buying patterns. For example, if the prices of certain foods escalate rapidly, consumers could substitute other foods to avoid the higher-priced items.

Second, the CPI does not measure the *standard of living*. That is, if an individual or family moves into a larger home and buys a better car, better furniture, and better clothing, this would require a larger outlay for living costs. This change in *lifestyle,* which would increase this household's living costs, would not be reflected in the annual CPI reading. Therefore, using this example, a household's living costs could increase substantially compared to a prior year, but it would have no relation to the percentage change in the cost of goods and services as measured by the CPI.

A Weighted Index

It is important to understand that the CPI is a *weighted index*. A weighted index is one in which all the items monitored for price changes are assigned a percentage amount (a weight). The total of the assigned percentage amounts (weights) is 100%. As a result, the changes in the items monitored are affected by the percentage weights assigned to each.

These weightings express the relative importance of items – that is the demand for certain items. A quick example: Since the food and beverage product group represents 17% of the total seven product groups, an annual increase within this category of 5.10% results in only a 0.87% (less than 1%) change in the overall annual CPI. This is calculated by multiplying 5.10% (.051) by 17% (.17), which equals .0087, or .87%.

Although this explanation of the weighting process is conceptually correct, the actual calculation of the CPI weighting procedure involves weighting individual items, not an overall product group. Therefore, the crucial point here is that percentage changes taking place in the items sampled are adjusted by their percentage weights. These weights are a direct result of an item's relative importance as calculated by the Department of Labor. Adding all of the individual weights for the items within a product group gives that group's percentage weight.

Table 3.3 *Annual CPI Reading*

	A	B	C	D
	Product Group	**% Weight**	**Annual Change**	**Weighted Change**
1	Food and Beverages	17.00%	5.10%	0.87%
2	Housing	42.00	4.00	1.68
3	Apparel and Upkeep	6.00	5.50	0.33
4	Transportation	17.00	3.00	0.51
5	Medical Care	7.00	6.90	0.48
6	Entertainment	4.00	4.60	0.18
7	Other Goods and Services	7.00	6.20	0.43
	Total	**100.00%**		**4.48%**

The percentage weights in column B are determined by the Department of Labor.

Let's take a look at Table 3.3. As we discussed earlier, the CPI is based on the sampling of many items purchased by consumers at the retail level. These items fall into the seven product groups in the table, and the approximate weight for each group is indicated in column B.

Column C shows the *annual change* occurring in the CPI product groups. The weighted change for each group, as shown in column D, is determined by multiplying the weights in column B by the annual percentage change in each product group (column C). The total weighted change in the table is 4.48%, which indicates the overall annual price change.

This is basically how the weighting process occurs except, as we mentioned earlier, weights are not assigned to each product group but to the items surveyed monthly within each product group. The price changes within each group are then averaged, resulting in the weighted percentage total for that group. As Table 3.3 illustrates, the percentage change in any particular group does *not* flow directly through to the CPI reading but is adjusted by its respective weight.

The Index Reading (Value)

To track changes in the price level over time as measured by the CPI, the Bureau of Labor Statistics calculates an annual index value. It is the change in the annual index value from year to year that reflects the percentage increase (inflation) or decrease (deflation) in the price level.

Table 3.4 *Index Readings (Values) 1982–1994*

A	B	C
Year	Inflation Rate	Index Value
1982		97.60
1983	3.80%	101.30
1984	3.90	105.30
1985	3.80	109.30
1986	1.10	110.50
1987	4.40	115.40
1988	4.40	120.50
1989	4.60	126.10
1990	6.10	133.80
1991	3.10	137.90
1992	2.90	141.90
1993	2.70	145.80
1994	2.70	149.70
Total	43.50%	

Source: U.S. Department of Labor, Bureau of Labor Statistics.

Table 3.4 shows the annual index values for the period from 1982 to 1994 (column C). The beginning period for this index has been numerically set at 100. Occasionally, the government resets the index reading to 100.00–termed rebasing. This has happened six times since the inception of the CPI. The last two rebasing periods occurred in 1967 and during 1982–1984. (Note the box around the years 1982–1984 in Table 3.4, showing the most recent period of time–the base year period–during which the index reading was reset to a base of 100. Also note that the index reading can be rebased to any given year–1967–or to a period of years–1982–1984.)

During the 1982–1984 period, the CPI reading ranged from 97.60 to 105.30. (It actually reached 100 between 1982 and 1983.) Based on the 1982–1984 rebasing, therefore, all readings before 1982 are now less than 100 and all readings after 1982–1984 are greater than 100.

The annual percentage changes between index values are the annual inflation or deflation rates measured by the CPI (column B). The most important point is that the index value in column C is increasing by the rate of inflation in column B (using the conversion formula we explained in Module 2). For instance, the 1983 index value of 101.30 was calculated by multiplying the 1982 index value of 97.60 by the 1983 conversion factor of 1.038. (The conversion factor was determined by dividing the 1983 inflation rate of 3.80% by 100 and then adding 1; refer back to Module 2 if you'd like a reminder of how this works and its significance). Therefore, it is obvious that the price level changes each year, based on the mathematics of compounding–that is, each year's inflation or deflation rates are applied to the prior year's index value by multiplication to arrive at the current year's index value.

The sum of the inflation rates during the 1982–1984 period (column C) is 43.5%. When the annual rates of inflation total 72, there will be a doubling in the index value; it will increase from its beginning 1982–1984 base-year-period reading of 100 to 200. (Always keep in mind that the rule of 72 is an estimate.)

Monthly Reporting of the CPI Reading

In order to give the government and the public timely information on consumer price levels, the CPI is calculated monthly and reported on business news programs and in business newspapers and magazines. One of the nation's most prominent business newspapers, *The Wall Street Journal,* lists the CPI reading during the third week after the close of each month. Table 3.5 shows the CPI reading in *The Wall Street Journal* for February 1995. This level of detail is not published every month.

Table 3.5 *Monthly CPI Reading (Expressed as a % change)*

A	B	C
Monthly CPI Reading	**Percent Change from**	
	January 1995	February 1994
All Items	0.30%	2.90%
Minus Food and Energy	0.30%	3.00%
Food and Beverage	0.30%	2.90%
Housing	0.30%	2.30%
Apparel	-0.60%	-1.00%
Transportation	0.40%	4.20%
Medical Care	0.30%	4.90%
Entertainment	0.20%	2.30%
Other	0.80%	4.60%
Cumulative CPI Reading	**1982 – 1984 = 100**	
All Urban Consumers (CPI-U)	150.90	2.90%
Urban Wage Earners and Clerical (CPI-W)	148.30	3.00%
Chicago	152.30	3.70%
Los Angeles	154.50	1.50%
New York	160.30	1.80%
Philadelphia	157.80	3.20%
San Francisco	150.50	2.10%
Dallas	143.30	2.90%
Detroit	147.30	4.00%
Houston	139.30	1.70%
Pittsburgh	147.30	3.30%

Table 3.5 lists the seven product groups of the CPI in the top portion of column A. The other two columns show the percentage changes for each group for the current month–in this case, from the previous month, January 1995, to February 1995 (column B)–and from the same month in the previous year, the year from February 1994 to February 1995 (column C).

Note that the monthly changes (column B, top portion) are very small and that the annual changes are much larger (column C, top portion). Although you should review the entire table, the most important information is the reading for "All Items." During February 1995, the monthly percent change for "All Items" was .30%, and for the twelve-month period since February 1994 it was 2.90%. Underneath the reading for "All Items" is the reading for "All Items Minus Food and Energy." Because the food and energy groups are highly volatile, the CPI reading is expressed twice each month: first, including food and energy, and second, without food and energy. We will be using the "All Items" reading.

The bottom portion of the table (column B) reports the CPI readings for major metropolitan areas of our country. Note that these are the *cumulative index readings* since the 1982–1984 rebasing to 100 (see Table 3.4) and that they vary from city to city. Also note that the annual percentage changes are listed beside the cumulative readings. You will see that the 2.90% change for the CPI-U in the bottom of the table is the same as the percentage change for "All Items" in the top of the table. This is because they are the same reading–the change in the consumer price index of urban consumers (CPI-U).

As we proceed, it is important that you recall the five-step economic model in Table 3.1. This model is the foundation for our financial planning system. We have just learned how to measure changes in living costs (step 4 of the five-step economic model). We'll now develop a budget for all the items of expense that fall under this classification, using the CPI's seven product groupings and percentage weights (see Table 3.3).

Developing a Budget for Living Costs

To develop a budget for living costs we must first decide how much after-tax income (step 3 of the five-step economic model) to allocate between living costs (step 4) and savings (step 5). After we've determined the total amount of after-tax income to spend on living costs, we must then allocate it among the various categories of expense that comprise living costs.

For example, let's develop a budget of living costs for a family earning a combined gross income of $40,000. Income taxes total $8,848. After-tax income is therefore $31,152. Let's say the family allocates 85% ($26,479) of its after-tax income to living costs and 15% ($4,673) to savings. (Note: A 15% savings rate is considered the minimum recommended savings rate when using this financial planning system.)

Table 3.6 *Annual Budget for Living Costs*

	A	B	C
	Product Group	**Percent**	**Dollar Amount**
1	Food and Beverages	17%	$ 4,501.43
2	Housing	42	11,121.18
3	Apparel and Upkeep	6	1,588.74
4	Transportation	17	4,501.43
5	Medical Care	7	1,853.53
6	Entertainment	4	1,059.16
7	Other Goods and Services	7	1,853.53
	Total	**100%**	**$26,479.00**

The percentage weights in column B are determined by the Department of Labor.

Table 3.6 distributes the $26,479 in living costs among the seven product groups of the CPI according to the percentage weightings in column B. The dollar amounts in column C show how much our hypothetical family can spend on each product group per year based on the percentage weights calculated by the Department of Labor. For instance, our family can spend $4,501.43 on food and beverages ($26,479 x 17%).

Now let's examine typical living costs for (1) a single person, (2) a married couple with children, and (3) a retired couple. These three different cost scenarios, which are shown in Table 3.7, illustrate how the items in each of the seven CPI product groups change as individuals move through the life cycle. Take a moment to compare them.

Table 3.7 *Typical Changing Budget for Living Costs*

	Single	Married	Retired
1	**Food and Beverages** Food	**Food and Beverages** Food	**Food and Beverages** Food
2	**Housing** Rent Personal Property Insurance	**Housing** Mortgage Real Estate Taxes Utilities/Household Expenses Homeowner's Insurance Personal Property Insurance	**Housing** Real Estate Taxes Utilities/Household Expenses Homeowner's Insurance Personal Property Insurance
3	**Apparel and Upkeep** Clothing	**Apparel and Upkeep** Clothing	**Apparel and Upkeep** Clothing
4	**Transportation** Auto Loan Payments Car Insurance Gasoline and Repairs Public Transportation	**Transportation** Auto Loan Payments Car Insurance Gasoline and Repairs Public Transportation	**Transportation** Car Insurance Gasoline and Repairs Public Transportation
5	**Medical Care** Medical Costs/Insurance Dental/Eye Examinations Prescription Drugs	**Medical Care** Medical Costs/Insurance Dental/Eye Examinations Prescription Drugs	**Medical Care** Medical Costs/Insurance Dental/Eye Examinations Prescription Drugs
6	**Entertainment** Vacations Fitness Programs Video Rentals	**Entertainment** Vacations Fitness Programs Video Rentals	**Entertainment** Vacations Fitness Programs Travel
7	**Other Goods and Services** Life Insurance Disability Insurance School Loans Credit Card Debt Charitable Giving Personal Care Items	**Other Goods and Services** Life Insurance Disability Insurance School Loans Credit Card Debt Charitable Giving Personal Care Items Children's Educational Costs	**Other Goods and Services** Charitable Giving Personal Care Items Support to Children Gifts to Grandchildren

The first column in Table 3.7 lists living cost categories for a single individual who pays rent. As you examine each of the living costs in each product group in this column, note that they are all variable, except for the auto and school loan payments, which we are assuming are fixed. Because the auto and school loan payments account for only a small portion of the total living costs, the living costs in this first example are greatly affected by inflationary increases. (Note that the amount owed for credit card debt in the other goods and services product group can vary widely.)

The second column shows living cost categories for a married couple with two children. (This column could also apply to a single parent with children or to an individual who has purchased a home. If it represents an individual with no children who has just purchased a home, it would, of course, exclude educational costs in the other goods and services product group).

Note that only a portion of the living cost items in each product group in this second scenario are variable–that is, only a portion will increase each year with inflation. The items that will not increase are the mortgage payment–a *large* portion of the budget–and the auto and school loan payments (assuming they are fixed). Therefore, even if inflation increases annually, only a portion of the living costs will be subject to these inflationary increases.

The third column lists living cost categories for a retired couple. Here, we can assume that the mortgage is paid off, along with any other type of installment debt (auto loans, school loans, and credit card debt, for example). All of the living costs in this third scenario are variable, which means that they will all increase each year with inflation. Comparing living costs in each product group from single to married to retired (reading from left to right) gives you a quick snapshot of the typical changes in the composition of a budget for living costs throughout a person's life cycle.

Now let's move on to determining your own living costs.

Determining Your Own Living Costs

Determining your own living costs is obviously a very personal thing, and can vary greatly from person to person. In general, however, living costs depend on four factors: (1) your stage in the life cycle; (2) your standard of living; (3) independent changes that arise in your living costs from year to year; and 4) the effects of inflation on the components of your budget that are variable (that increase with inflation annually). These four factors are illustrated in Table 3.8. Let's discuss each factor.

Table 3.8 *Factors Affecting Living Costs*

Living Costs Depend On:
1. Stage in the Life Cycle
2. Standard of Living
3. Independent Changes
4. Inflation

The cost components of an individual's budget vary according to that person's stage in the life cycle–discussed earlier and illustrated by Table 3.7. Clearly, a young, single individual's budget for living costs will differ substantially from that of a married household with children or a retired couple. These differences arise because of different sets of needs.

The second factor in determining your own living costs is the standard of living you require within each stage of the life cycle. Once the three most important of the seven product groups of the CPI are satisfied–food, shelter, and clothing–you can enhance your standard of living by increasing the amount you spend on these and the remaining four product groups–transportation, medical care, entertainment, and other goods and services.

Let's look at an example using a young single individual. At one extreme is a person who lives lavishly in a penthouse apartment, eats out every night, dresses in the latest fashions, and drives the best sports car available. His medical coverage is provided by his employer, and he involves himself in a wide variety of entertainment activities.

At the other extreme is the person who is employed only part-time, shares an average apartment with two other individuals, eats in every night, buys all his clothes at discount outlets, and uses public transportation. He has no medical insurance because typically it is not provided for part-time employees. His entertainment is limited to long walks in the park, reading the newspaper, watching television, and catching an occasional bargain matinee. Obviously, there is a big difference between these two extremes, with plenty of room for adjustments at each stage of the life cycle.

The third factor in determining your living costs is the changes which occur that are independent of the rate of inflation. These changes can happen at any stage of the life cycle. One such change that would alter your budget for living costs is the purchase of a home. Your budget for living costs would then have to account for the mortgage payment, real estate taxes, and homeowner's insurance, whereas prior to the purchase, only your rent payment and insurance on personal items would have been necessary budgeted items.

Independent changes could also include the costs of having a child, college tuition costs, or unforeseen medical expenses not covered by insurance. Any of these costs would require an adjustment in living costs not only for the year in which they occurred, but also for years to come. (Note that independent changes may also have a positive impact on a budget for living costs. For example, paying off a mortgage, car, or school loan would actually *lower* your annual living costs.)

Finally, the fourth factor in determining living costs is inflation as measured by the Consumer Price Index. After identifying your stage in the life cycle, your standard of living, and the effect of independent changes from year to year, you then need to adjust for inflation. Keep in mind that not all components in a budget for living costs increase annually with inflation. For example, a fixed car loan payment, fixed school loan payment, or a fixed mortgage payment remain constant from year to year, despite the rate of inflation. On the other hand, the cost of food, rental costs on an apartment, clothing, and medical costs all increase with inflation.

In summary, the annual inflation reading as measured by the CPI does not measure your living costs or your standard of living. Furthermore, it does not account for where you are in the life cycle; nor does it account for independent changes that occur in your living costs. What the CPI does measure is the *average* change in prices over time.

Purchasing Power of the Dollar

In Module 2 we discussed the two doublings that have occurred in living costs, using 1949 as the base year: the first occurred in 1974 and the second in 1982. We also pointed out that we are on our way to a third doubling in living costs.

What is important to understand is that every time living costs double, the *purchasing power* of a dollar is diminished. Analyzing the dollar's purchasing power in relation to a base period determines how much that power is diminished. Using 1949 as our base year indicates that the purchasing power of a dollar decreased to 50 cents in 1974 (at the first doubling) and then decreased again to 25 cents in 1982 (at the second doubling). When the third doubling occurs, the purchasing power of a 1949 dollar will have decreased to 12.5 cents. These reductions in purchasing power are illustrated in Table 3.9.

Table 3.9 *Purchasing Power of a 1949 Dollar*

A	B
Year	**Value of the Dollar**
1949	1.00
1974	0.50
1982	0.25
3rd Doubling	0.125

It is important to keep in mind these twin concepts of doublings in living costs and reduced purchasing power of the dollar. Understanding this becomes important in Module 6 when you learn to set target financial amounts which are high enough to offset the effects of inflation so that you achieve your financial goals.

Module 4 Taxation

In Module 4, "Taxation," we will discuss the five basic categories of taxes that affect the financial planning process: (1) income taxes, (2) sales taxes, (3) license taxes, (4) property taxes, and (5) transfer taxes (see Table 4.1).

Table 4.1 *The Five Categories of Taxes*

1	2	3	4	5
Income Taxes	**Sales Taxes**	**License Taxes**	**Property Taxes**	**Transfer Taxes**
1. Federal 2. FICA 3. State 4. Local	Taxes on Purchases, Including Excise Taxes	Taxes for Revenue-Raising or Administration of Laws	Real and Personal Property Taxes	Gift and Estate Taxes

Income taxes, the first category of taxes, are made up of these four types of taxes: (1) federal income tax, (2) FICA tax (social security and medicare), (3) state income tax, and (4) local income tax. Although not shown in the table, other forms of taxes based on income do exist and therefore would be classified as income taxes. These vary from state to state and from locality to locality. Consequently, we mention them here so that you will remember to include them in your plan if you are subject to these additional forms of income tax. No further mention of them will be made in the text.

Sales taxes, the second category, are composed of taxes on purchases, including excise taxes. License taxes, the third category, are taxes which collect revenue in conjunction with the administration of laws. Property taxes, the fourth category, are made up of real and personal property taxes. Transfer taxes, the fifth and final category, are composed of gift and estate taxes.

In planning your financial future, it is important to keep in consideration all of the taxes in Table 4.1. You are faced with these five categories of taxes throughout your lifetime and successful financial planning requires an understanding of each category.

Table 4.2 *The Five-Step Economic Model*

Let's take another look at the five-step economic model that we introduced in Module 3. This model allows you to understand where your money comes from and where it is going (see Table 4.2). Think of the model as a road map to guide you through the financial planning process. To monitor the transition from gross income (step 1) to after-tax income (step 3), you must fully understand the mechanics of income taxes (step 2).

Therefore, we will now examine the four types of income taxes involved in the transition from gross income to after-tax income. Let's start with the first type–federal income taxes–by examining the U.S. individual income tax return.

Understanding the U.S. Individual Income Tax Return

You may find it helpful at this point to review the federal individual income tax return so that you, as a taxpayer, can see the big picture of federal income taxation. The federal government raises its money primarily by taxing the *earnings of individuals* through the individual income tax and through FICA taxes (social security and medicare taxes). Other sources of revenue for the federal government are corporate income taxes and miscellaneous taxes that include excise taxes, customs taxes, estate taxes, gift taxes and borrowing to cover the deficit.

Table 4.3 lists the 13 sections of the individual tax return form (Form 1040). Note that the section titles in this table do not exactly match the section headings on an actual return. This is because we have modified the table headings to make them easier to understand. We will not be discussing the Form 1040 A or 1040 EZ, which are shorter versions of the Form 1040. Once you understand the Form 1040, it will be easy to understand the shorter forms, 1040 A and 1040 EZ, if you use either of those forms.

Table 4.3 *The U.S. Individual Income Tax Return (Form 1040)*

Section 1	Name and Mailing Address	Top of Form
Section 2	Filing Status	Lines 1–5
Section 3	Exemptions	Lines 6a–6e
Section 4	Total Income	Lines 7–22
Section 5	Less Adjustments to Income	Lines 23a–30
Section 6	Equals Adjusted Gross Income (AGI)	Line 31
Section 7	Tax Computation (Begin with AGI)	Lines 32–40
	Less Standard Deduction or Itemized Deductions	Line 34
	Less Personal Exemption Amount	Line 36
	Equals Taxable Income (TI)	Line 37
	Calculation of Tax Due on Taxable Income	Lines 38–40
Section 8	Less Tax Credits	Lines 41–46
Section 9	Addition of Other Taxes	Lines 47–54
Section 10	Less Payments	Lines 55–61
Section 11	Amount You Owe (Refund)	Lines 62–66
Section 12	Signature	End of Form
Section 13	Paid Preparer's Use Only	End of Form

Take a minute now to examine the various sections of the 1040 return. By simply studying this table, you will quickly see how each section relates to the next. Now we'll discuss each section, one at a time. (Note that we are using *the 1995 federal income tax form* as our reference.)

Section 1: Name and Mailing Address

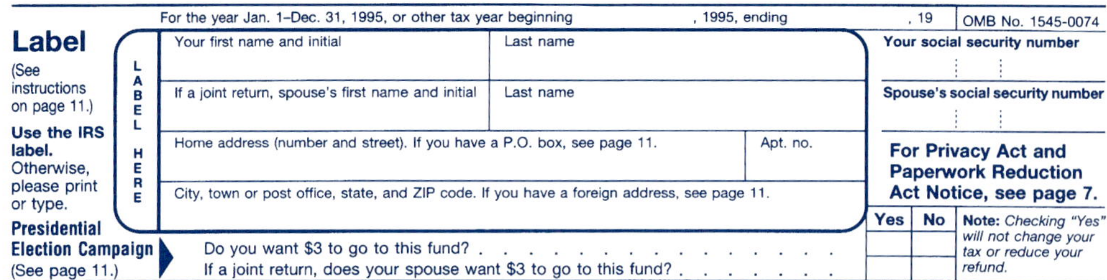

For the year Jan. 1–Dec. 31, 1995, or other tax year beginning , 1995, ending , 19 | OMB No. 1545-0074

Label
(See instructions on page 11.)
Use the IRS label. Otherwise, please print or type.

LABEL HERE

Your first name and initial	Last name	Your social security number
If a joint return, spouse's first name and initial	Last name	Spouse's social security number
Home address (number and street). If you have a P.O. box, see page 11.	Apt. no.	**For Privacy Act and Paperwork Reduction Act Notice, see page 7.**
City, town or post office, state, and ZIP code. If you have a foreign address, see page 11.		

Presidential Election Campaign (See page 11.)

	Yes	No	**Note:** *Checking "Yes" will not change your tax or reduce your refund.*
Do you want $3 to go to this fund?			
If a joint return, does your spouse want $3 to go to this fund?			

The first section is used primarily for recording the taxpayer's name(s), address, and social security number(s). At the bottom of the first section, you are asked if you would like to give to the presidential election campaign. Congress has set up this fund to help pay for candidates' campaign costs, thereby reducing their dependence on large contributions.

Section 2: Filing Status

Filing Status
(See page 11.)
Check only one box.

1	☐	Single
2	☐	Married filing joint return (even if only one had income)
3	☐	Married filing separate return. Enter spouse's social security no. above and full name here. ▶ ________
4	☐	Head of household (with qualifying person). (See page 12.) If the qualifying person is a child but not your dependent, enter this child's name here. ▶ ________
5	☐	Qualifying widow(er) with dependent child (year spouse died ▶ 19). (See page 12.)

The second section is used for recording your filing status (lines 1-5). There are five different filing classifications, as follows: (1) single, (2) married filing a joint return, (3) married filing a separate return, (4) head of household, and (5) qualifying widow(er) with dependent child. (Note that in subsequent parts of Form 1040, the "married filing a joint return" classification is often combined with qualifying widow(er) with dependent child–also referred to as surviving spouse with dependent child.)

Section 3: Exemptions

Exemptions
(See page 12.)

If more than six dependents, see page 13.

6a ☐ **Yourself.** If your parent (or someone else) can claim you as a dependent on his or her tax return, **do not** check box 6a. But be sure to check the box on line 33b on page 2 . } **No. of boxes checked on 6a and 6b** ____

b ☐ **Spouse** . . . .

c **Dependents:**

(1) First name	Last name	(2) Dependent's social security number. If born in 1995, see page 13.	(3) Dependent's relationship to you	(4) No. of months lived in your home in 1995

No. of your children on 6c who:
- **lived with you** ____
- **didn't live with you due to divorce or separation (see page 14)** ____

Dependents on 6c not entered above ____

d If your child didn't live with you but is claimed as your dependent under a pre-1985 agreement, check here ▶ ☐

e Total number of exemptions claimed . . . . **Add numbers entered on lines above ▶** ☐

The "Exemptions" section (lines 6a–6e) is for recording the total number of exemptions you can claim on your tax return. Exemptions (beyond yourself) are individuals who are somehow dependent on you, the taxpayer, and meet all of the following five tests: (1) the relationship test, (2) the married person test, (3) the citizen or resident test, (4) the income test, and (5) the support test. (See the Form 1040 instruction booklet for an explanation of these requirements.) For each exemption allowed, you can deduct $2,500 on line 36 of your 1995 Form 1040 tax return.

Section 4: Total Income

Income

Attach Copy B of your Forms W-2, W-2G, and 1099-R here.

If you did not get a W-2, see page 14.

Enclose, but do not attach, your payment and payment voucher. See page 33.

7	Wages, salaries, tips, etc. Attach Form(s) W-2	7	
8a	**Taxable** interest income (see page 15). Attach Schedule B if over $400	8a	
b	**Tax-exempt** interest (see page 15). DON'T include on line 8a [8b]		
9	Dividend income. Attach Schedule B if over $400	9	
10	Taxable refunds, credits, or offsets of state and local income taxes (see page 15)	10	
11	Alimony received	11	
12	Business income or (loss). Attach Schedule C or C-EZ	12	
13	Capital gain or (loss). If required, attach Schedule D (see page 16)	13	
14	Other gains or (losses). Attach Form 4797	14	
15a	Total IRA distributions [15a] **b** Taxable amount (see page 16)	15b	
16a	Total pensions and annuities [16a] **b** Taxable amount (see page 16)	16b	
17	Rental real estate, royalties, partnerships, S corporations, trusts, etc. Attach Schedule E	17	
18	Farm income or (loss). Attach Schedule F	18	
19	Unemployment compensation (see page 17)	19	
20a	Social security benefits [20a] **b** Taxable amount (see page 18)	20b	
21	Other income. List type and amount—see page 18	21	
22	Add the amounts in the far right column for lines 7 through 21. This is your **total income** ▶	22	

The fourth section is "Total Income" (lines 7-22). Although there are 15 components to this section, they are easily divided into four main groupings: (1) *earnings* from employment or self-employment, (2) *return on investments* (for example, interest on savings accounts and dividends on stocks), (3) *capital gains or losses* on various types of property which you owned and sold (for example, from the sale of stocks, bonds, or real estate for more or less than the price you paid for them), and (4) *payments received* (alimony, IRA distributions, unemployment compensation, social security benefits, rental payments, royalties, refunds and earnings from partnerships, estates, and trusts).

Recap: It is important that you get the big picture of where we are headed. We have just discussed the various sources of income reported on Form 1040. At this point, your goal is to reduce as much as legally possible the amount of income on which your tax liability will be calculated in order to minimize your federal income taxes. Therefore, as you proceed through the remainder of the federal tax return, think of going through a tunnel that gets progressively narrower. As you enter the tunnel, you do so with *total (gross) income*. When you exit the tunnel, you do so with *taxable income* against which your federal tax liability is calculated.

Section 5: Less Adjustments to Income

Adjustments to Income					
23a	Your IRA deduction (see page 19)	23a			
b	Spouse's IRA deduction (see page 19)	23b			
24	Moving expenses. Attach Form 3903 or 3903-F	24			
25	One-half of self-employment tax	25			
26	Self-employed health insurance deduction (see page 21)	26			
27	Keogh & self-employed SEP plans. If SEP, check ► ☐	27			
28	Penalty on early withdrawal of savings	28			
29	Alimony paid. Recipient's SSN ►	29			
30	Add lines 23a through 29. These are your **total adjustments** ►			30	

The fifth section, "Adjustments to Income" (lines 23a-30), consists of items that reduce your total (gross) income on a dollar-for-dollar basis (deductions). The more deductions that you can take advantage of in this section, the more you will reduce the amount of taxable income on which your tax liability is calculated. The "Adjustments to Income" section includes IRA deductions (for specified ranges of income), moving expenses, self-employment taxes, self-employment health insurance costs, self-employed retirement plan contributions, penalties for early withdrawal of savings, and alimony paid.

Section 6: Equals Adjusted Gross Income (AGI)

Adjusted Gross Income				
31	Subtract line 30 from line 22. This is your **adjusted gross income**. If less than $26,673 and a child lived with you (less than $9,230 if a child didn't live with you), see "Earned Income Credit" on page 27 ►	31		

"Adjusted Gross Income" (line 31), the sixth section, is the net amount of total (gross) income you have after deductions (gross income minus adjustments to income). Note that your adjusted gross income will be used in subsequent parts of the return to set limits on allowable medical deductions and allowable casualty and theft loss deductions, to set maximum limits on allowable charitable contribution deductions, to determine if your contributions to an IRA are deductible, and to calculate the point beyond which your personal exemption and itemized deduction amounts are phased out (reduced). Consequently, a lower AGI figure can result in a larger deduction.

Section 7: Tax Computation (Begin with AGI): Less Standard Deduction or Itemized Deductions

Tax Computation

(See page 23.)

32 Amount from line 31 (adjusted gross income) 32

33a Check if: ☐ **You** were 65 or older, ☐ Blind; ☐ **Spouse** was 65 or older, ☐ Blind.
Add the number of boxes checked above and enter the total here . . . . ▶ 33a

b If your parent (or someone else) can claim you as a dependent, check here . ▶ 33b ☐

c If you are married filing separately and your spouse itemizes deductions or you are a dual-status alien, see page 23 and check here . . . . ▶ 33c ☐

34 Enter the **larger** of your:
- **Itemized deductions** from Schedule A, line 28, **OR**
- **Standard deduction** shown below for your filing status. **But if you checked any box on line 33a or b,** go to page 23 to find your standard deduction. If you checked **box 33c,** your standard deduction is zero.
  - Single—$3,900 • Married filing jointly or Qualifying widow(er)—$6,550
  - Head of household—$5,750 • Married filing separately—$3,275

34

35 Subtract line 34 from line 32 35

36 If line 32 is $86,025 or less, multiply $2,500 by the total number of exemptions claimed on line 6e. If line 32 is over $86,025, see the worksheet on page 23 for the amount to enter . 36

If you want the IRS to figure your tax, see page 35.

37 **Taxable income.** Subtract line 36 from line 35. If line 36 is more than line 35, enter -0- . 37

38 Tax. Check if from **a** ☐ Tax Table, **b** ☐ Tax Rate Schedules, **c** ☐ Capital Gain Tax Worksheet, or **d** ☐ Form 8615 (see page 24). Amount from Form(s) 8814 ▶ **e** ______ 38

39 Additional taxes. Check if from **a** ☐ Form 4970 **b** ☐ Form 4972 39

40 Add lines 38 and 39 . . . . ▶ 40

The seventh section is "Tax Computation" (lines 32-40). The next step in reducing your gross income is to *subtract* the amount which you recorded on line 34 – either the standard deduction or the total of your itemized deductions (whichever is greater) – from your adjusted gross income (line 32). The *standard deduction,* which is based on a taxpayer's filing status and determined by the IRS, provides a reduction to an individual's gross income. The standard deduction amounts for the 1995 tax year are shown in Table 4.4.

Table 4.4 *1995 Standard Deduction Amounts*

Filing Status	Standard Deduction
Married Filing Jointly or Qualifying Widower	$6,550
Head of Household	5,750
Single	3,900
Married Filing Separately	3,275

Table 4.4 lists the standard deduction amounts for the different filing status classifications. All you need to know right now about the standard deduction is that it is largest for married persons filing jointly and that it decreases for the other categories, with married persons filing separately having the smallest deduction.

Sometimes a taxpayer does not use the standard deduction because he or she can obtain a greater deduction by itemizing. Expenses that qualify as *itemized deductions,* which are calculated using Schedule A of the tax return, consist primarily of these personal expenditure items: medical and dental expenses, state and local income taxes, real and personal property taxes, home mortgage interest, investment interest expense, charitable contributions, casualty and theft losses, and job-related expenses. Most itemized deductions are subject to limitations (listed on Schedule A). There are also additional standard deduction amounts for individuals who are elderly (over age 65) or blind.

If the total of your itemized deductions is greater than the standard deduction to which you are entitled, you will want to use the itemized deduction amount instead of the standard deduction amount. Remember, the goal is to reduce your AGI by as much as legally possible.

Section 7: Tax Computation: Less Personal Exemption Amount

Personal exemptions (line 36) represent the second category of reductions that are applied against AGI. There are three kinds of personal exemptions: (1) the taxpayer's exemption for himself or herself, (2) the exemption for the taxpayer's spouse if the taxpayer is married, and (3) the exemptions for the taxpayer's dependents. As we discussed earlier (see "Section 3: Exemptions"), a deduction of $2,500 for each exemption claimed for the 1995 tax year can be applied against AGI using this formula:

Number of Exemptions × $2,500 = Total Exemption Amount Deductible

Section 7: Tax Computation: Equals Taxable Income (TI)

After subtracting the greater of the standard deduction or the total of your itemized deductions and the amount for personal exemptions (lines 32-36) from your adjusted gross income (line 31), the net result is your taxable income (line 37). Taxable income is used in conjunction with the tax rate tables or tax rate schedules to determine the amount of federal income tax due at this point in the tax computation process.

Section 7: Tax Computation:
Calculation of Tax Due on Taxable Income

The next step is to calculate the amount of tax (lines 37-40). If your taxable income is less than $100,000, you can refer to the applicable section of the *tax tables*. If your taxable income is $100,000 or greater, you must use the *tax rate schedules*. Once the federal tax is calculated, there are four more steps to finalizing your return: accounting for tax credits, adding other taxes, accounting for payments already made during the year, and determining the amount you owe or the refund due you.

Section 8: Less Tax Credits

Credits	41	Credit for child and dependent care expenses. Attach Form 2441	41		
	42	Credit for the elderly or the disabled. Attach Schedule R . .	42		
(See page 24.)	43	Foreign tax credit. Attach Form 1116	43		
	44	Other credits (see page 25). Check if from **a** ☐ Form 3800 **b** ☐ Form 8396 **c** ☐ Form 8801 **d** ☐ Form (specify)_____	44		
	45	Add lines 41 through 44			45
	46	Subtract line 45 from line 40. If line 45 is more than line 40, enter -0- . . . . ▶			46

Section 8 is "Tax Credits" (lines 41-46). The most important feature of tax credits is that they are dollar-for-dollar reductions against your *tax liability* (the amount of tax you owe). Let's look at a quick example. If you owe $2,000 in federal income taxes, determined by using the tax rate table to calculate your tax liability, a $200 tax credit would reduce the tax to $1,800. *Therefore, tax credits are dollar-for-dollar reductions to your tax liability, not to your taxable income.*

Tax credits are provided primarily for child and dependent care expenses, the elderly or disabled, foreign taxes paid, investments in low-income housing, certain real estate rehabilitation expenditures, and qualified research expenditures. In contrast, deductions (reductions to gross income) reduce the amount of taxable income against which you calculate the tax in three potential ways: via a standard or itemized deduction (line 34), a personal exemption amount (line 6) and adjustments to income (lines 23–30).

Because the tax credits reduce your actual tax liability, thay have a greater impact than deductions on the amount of tax you owe. As a hypothetical example, for someone in a 33⅓% tax bracket who owes $300 in federal taxes, a $100 tax credit is *three times more* valuable than $100 of deductions. This is because the tax credit reduces the tax liability from $300 to $200, while the deduction lowers the tax liability by only $33 (from $300 to $267).

Section 9: Addition of Other Taxes

Other Taxes (See page 25.)				
	47	Self-employment tax. Attach Schedule SE	47	
	48	Alternative minimum tax. Attach Form 6251	48	
	49	Recapture taxes. Check if from a ☐ Form 4255 b ☐ Form 8611 c ☐ Form 8828	49	
	50	Social security and Medicare tax on tip income not reported to employer. Attach Form 4137	50	
	51	Tax on qualified retirement plans, including IRAs. If required, attach Form 5329	51	
	52	Advance earned income credit payments from Form W-2	52	
	53	Household employment taxes. Attach Schedule H	53	
	54	Add lines 46 through 53. This is your **total tax** ▶	54	

After you have subtracted tax credits from your tax liability, other taxes–Section 9 (lines 47–54)–may need to be added. Other taxes include self-employment tax, the alternative minimum tax, recapture taxes, social security and Medicare tax on tip income not reported to an employer, tax on qualified retirement plans (including IRAs), advance earned-income credit payments from Form W-2, and household employment taxes. Line 54 indicates your total tax, which may increase after adding other taxes.

Section 10: Less Payments

Payments (Attach Forms W-2, W-2G, and 1099-R on the front.)						
	55	Federal income tax withheld. If any is from Form(s) 1099, check ▶ ☐	55			
	56	1995 estimated tax payments and amount applied from 1994 return	56			
	57	**Earned income credit.** Attach Schedule EIC if you have a qualifying child. Nontaxable earned income: amount ▶ and type ▶	57			
	58	Amount paid with Form 4868 (extension request)	58			
	59	Excess social security and RRTA tax withheld (see page 32)	59			
	60	Other payments. Check if from a ☐ Form 2439 b ☐ Form 4136	60			
	61	Add lines 55 through 60. These are your **total payments** ▶			61	

Section 10, "Payments" (lines 55–61), reports the various forms of payments you have already made against the total tax due from line 54. The payments, which will in effect reduce your total tax amount, consist of federal income tax withheld, estimated tax payments made in the current year and any amount applied from the prior year's return, earned-income credit (which is not in actuality a payment), amounts paid with Form 4868 (extension request), excess social security and railroad retirement tax withheld, and other payments. The total of these payment amounts is recorded on line 61.

Section 11: Amount You Owe/Refund

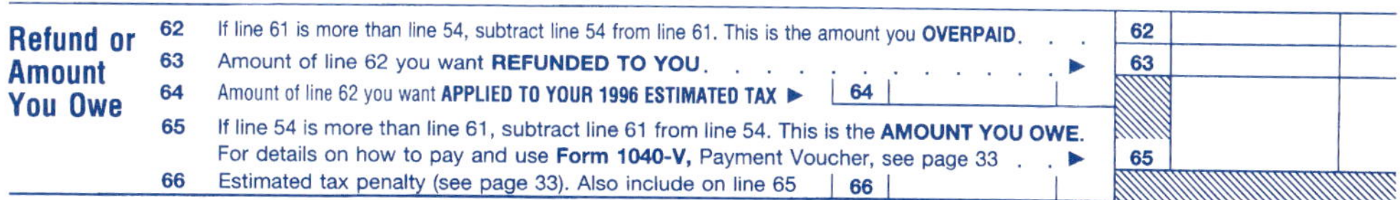

Refund or Amount You Owe			
	62	If line 61 is more than line 54, subtract line 54 from line 61. This is the amount you **OVERPAID**	62
	63	Amount of line 62 you want **REFUNDED TO YOU** ▶	63
	64	Amount of line 62 you want **APPLIED TO YOUR 1996 ESTIMATED TAX** ▶ 64	
	65	If line 54 is more than line 61, subtract line 61 from line 54. This is the **AMOUNT YOU OWE**. For details on how to pay and use **Form 1040-V,** Payment Voucher, see page 33 ▶	65
	66	Estimated tax penalty (see page 33). Also include on line 65 66	

The 11th section, "Amount You Owe/Refund" (lines 62–66), shows the amount you owe the federal government or the refund due you. In either case, the amount is determined by comparing what you owe against what you have already paid. If you owe tax to the federal government, it must be paid by the stipulated deadline. If money is owed to you, the government will process the return and forward that amount to you—assuming the calculations are correct.

Section 12: Signature

Sign Here

Keep a copy of this return for your records.

Under penalties of perjury, I declare that I have examined this return and accompanying schedules and statements, and to the best of my knowledge and belief, they are true, correct, and complete. Declaration of preparer (other than taxpayer) is based on all information of which preparer has any knowledge.

Your signature	Date	Your occupation
Spouse's signature. If a joint return, BOTH must sign.	Date	Spouse's occupation

Section 12 requires you and your spouse (if applicable) to sign and date the return and list your occupations. By signing the return, you are declaring that the information contained in the form is accurate. A copy of the return should be kept for your records.

Section 13: Paid Preparer's Use Only

Paid Preparer's Use Only

Preparer's signature	Date	Check if self-employed ☐	Preparer's social security no.
Firm's name (or yours if self-employed) and address		EIN	
		ZIP code	

The last section of the return is to be filled out by the person or entity who actually prepared the return if you did not do so yourself. The paid preparer is required to sign his or her name (or the entity's name), address, social security number (or employer identification number if an entity) and the date.

Recap: Congratulations. You have just made your way through the individual income tax return. Although there are many supporting schedules to this return, they all lead back to Form 1040. We will now explain how the federal income tax system is a progressive tax system.

Understanding Tax Brackets

Let's discuss the federal income tax rate structure. The federal income tax rate structure is progressive—that is, the more you earn, the higher the rate will be that is levied on your taxable income.

There were five tax brackets for the tax year 1995: the 15% tax bracket, the 28% tax bracket, the 31% tax bracket, the 36% tax bracket, and the 39.6% tax bracket (see Table 4.5). Whether you are single, married filing separately, or the head of a household in 1995, you are still faced with the same five tax brackets. The only differences are the threshold amounts (the maximum taxable income level in each bracket before a taxpayer moves into the next bracket). We will illustrate the tax rates for married filing jointly or qualifying widower.

Table 4.5 *The 1995 Tax Brackets*

A	B	C	D
Bracket	**Year**	**If Taxable Income Is**	**The Tax Is**
1	1995	Not over $39,000	15% of Taxable Income
2	1995	Over $39,000 but not over $94,250	$5,850 Plus 28% of the Amount over $39,000
3	1995	Over $94,250 but not over $143,600	$21,320 Plus 31% of the Amount over $94,250
4	1995	Over $143,600 but not over $256,500	$36,618.50 Plus 36% of the Amount over $143,600
5	1995	Over $256,500	$77,262.50 Plus 39.6% of the Amount over $256,500

Remember, the federal income tax is calculated against *taxable income* (gross income reduced by deductions). Taxable income not exceeding $39,000 is taxed at a flat 15% rate. This is the first tax bracket.

Taxable income exceeding $39,000 but not over $94,250 is taxed at a flat tax of $5,850 (15% of $39,000) plus 28% of the excess amount over $39,000 but not over $94,250. This is the second tax bracket.

Taxable income over $94,250 but not over $143,600 is taxed at a flat tax of $21,320 (based on the taxable income of the first two tax brackets) plus 31% of the excess over $94,250 but not over $143,600. This is the third tax bracket.

In the fourth tax bracket, taxable income exceeding $143,600 but not over $256,500 is taxed at a flat tax of $36,618.50 (based on the taxable income in the first three tax brackets) plus 36% of the excess amount over $143,600 but not over $256,500.

Finally, taxable income over $256,500 is taxed at a flat tax of $77,262.50 (based on the taxable income of the first four tax brackets) plus 39.6% on the excess amount over $256,500. This is the fifth tax bracket.

Summary of Tax Brackets

Table 4.5 leads us to three important points:

(1) First, the federal income tax is a progressive tax. As we explained before, this simply means that the more you earn *(the higher your taxable income)*, the higher the tax rate applied (and thus the greater the amount of tax owed (before accounting for credits, additional taxes or prepayments). See Sections 8, 9, and 10.

(2) Second, there are four threshold amounts (again, a threshold amount is the maximum taxable income level in each bracket before a taxpayer jumps to the next bracket): $39,000, $94,250, $143,600, and $256,500 (for married filing jointly or a qualifying widower for the tax year 1995).

(3) Third, because the federal income tax structure is progressive and the taxpayer pays different percentage amounts of tax on different levels of taxable income, this leads to the concept of an *average federal tax rate* (also called an effective tax rate).

Calculating Federal Tax on $256,500 of Taxable Income

We will now illustrate how to calculate the tax due on taxable income of $256,500 for a married couple filing jointly or a qualifying widower for the 1995 tax year. This calculation will involve using four of the five tax brackets. The concepts we'll explain will work exactly the same way in the single, married filing separately, or head of household filing status. Furthermore, once you grasp how this process works, you can apply it to changing future tax rates and bracket amounts.

Before we learn the mechanics of income taxation at the federal level, let's quickly describe Table 4.6 which appears on page 52. Column B lists the ranges of taxable income for the first four tax brackets. Column C shows the taxable income within each range. Column D gives the marginal tax rates that apply to the taxable income within each range in column C. The dollar amount of tax due for each range of taxable income is indicated in column E (column C multiplied by column D). Column F, "Cumulative Tax," is the total of the incremental tax amounts in column E. Column G, "Average Tax Rate," is column F divided by the *threshold* amount in each taxable income range.

Table 4.6 *Federal Tax on Taxable Income of $256,500*

A	B	C	D	E	F	G
Tax Brackets	Taxable Income Range	Taxable Income	Marginal Tax Rate	Incremental Tax	Cumulative Tax	Average Tax Rate
1	$0 – $39,000	$ 39,000	15%	$ 5,850.00	$ 5,850.00	15.00%
2	$39,000 – $94,250	$ 55,250	28%	$ 15,470.00	$21,320.00	22.62%
3	$94,250 – $143,600	$ 49,350	31%	$ 15,298.50	$36,618.50	25.50%
4	$143,600 – $256,500	$ 112,900	36%	$ 40,644.00	$77,262.50	30.12%
Total		**$256,500**		**$77,262.50**		**30.12%**

As you'll note from examining the table, once a taxpayer moves into a higher tax bracket, it is only *the taxable income exceeding the prior bracket amount* that is taxed at the next highest tax rate. This brings about an average or effective federal tax rate (see column G).

Column F, "Cumulative Tax," is the total of the tax amounts due in column E. In column E, the tax (due of $5,850 on the first $39,000 of taxable income) is based on a 15% tax rate. The next $15,470 of tax (due on taxable income over $39,000 but not beyond $94,250) is based on a 28% tax rate, and so on. The total of tax amounts due in column E is $77,262.50 (see column F for cumulative total). Dividing $77,262.50 by $256,500 equals 30.12%. This is the average (effective) tax rate on $256,500 of taxable income. Note that the average (effective) tax rate (column G) is not increasing as fast as the marginal tax rate (column D). This is because the tax rate increase *at each threshold amount* applies only to the amount of taxable income over the threshold amount.

Table 4.7 illustrates that, even though the marginal tax rate increases at each threshold amount, the average tax rate increases at a somewhat lesser rate. This table is simply a graphic representation of columns D ("Marginal Tax Rate") and G ("Average Tax Rate") in Table 4.6.

Table 4.7 *Marginal versus Average Tax Rates*

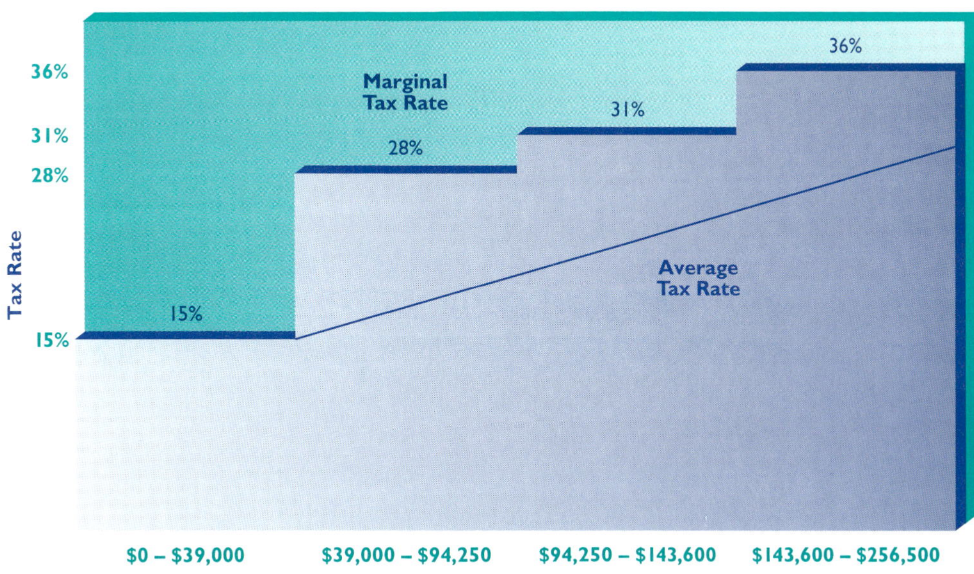

Tax Rate Schedules

Table 4.6 calculates the federal income tax due by using the taxable income ranges and marginal tax brackets *cumulatively*. This means that the tax amount owed from a lower bracket is added to the tax from the next higher bracket.

Each year, when you receive tax return Form 1040 from the Internal Revenue Service, there is one important piece of information that you should investigate. Find the tax rate schedules that summarize the many pages of tax tables into one table for each filing classification. This table will enable you to quickly determine the tax rate that applies to each bracket of *taxable income based on your filing status.* (Portions of Table 4.6 are taken from the 1995 tax rate schedules.)

In Form 1040 there are two methods to determine the tax due, depending on the amount of taxable income. For 1995, taxable income of less than $100,000 is calculated using the tax rate tables. For taxable income of $100,000 and above, the tax rate schedules are used. *The tax rate schedules, although used for taxable income amounts of $100,000 and over, illustrate all taxable income levels.*

Each year, therefore, after you determine your filing status and taxable income, you can *approximate* the tax due using the tax rate schedules. Using the tax rate schedules to calculate the tax enables you to see the threshold amounts and determine the amount of tax you are paying in each bracket of your taxable income. By comparing the current year's tax brackets with the prior year's, you will be alerted immediately to changes in bracket amounts which may affect your tax profile.

Let's now discuss FICA, state, and local income taxes–the second, third, and fourth types of income taxes, respectively.

FICA Taxes

FICA taxes have two components: social security tax (for retirement and disability benefits) and medicare tax (for health care benefits). FICA taxes are calculated only against employee wages (gross *earned* income).

For the tax year 1995, the FICA tax rate is 7.65%–a 6.20% tax for social security and a 1.45% tax for medicare. The 6.20% social security portion is calculated against only the first $61,200 of employee wages. No social security tax is levied against employee wages exceeding $61,200.

The $61,200 is the ceiling amount against which the social security portion of FICA tax is applied. As a result, the 1995 maximum social security portion of FICA tax that an employed individual would pay is $3,794.40 (6.20% x $61,200). Taxable wages exceeding the $61,200 ceiling are not taxed. Therefore, the social security portion of FICA tax actually becomes regressive once the taxpayer surpasses the ceiling amount. The 1.45% medicare portion, on the other hand, is calculated against the total amount of employee wages. There is no ceiling amount.

FICA taxes are paid at both the employee and the employer level. The total FICA tax rate for 1995 is actually 15.30%–7.65% paid by the employer and 7.65% paid by the employee. For the employer, the FICA tax is a payroll tax calculated against the total payroll. For the employee, the tax is applied against his or her individual wages (gross earned income). Self-employed individuals must pay the full 15.30% because there is no employer with whom to split the tax.

For the self-employed, the FICA tax is broken down as follows: a 12.40% OASDI tax (old age, survivors, and disability insurance tax—the equivalent of the social security tax levied on employers and employees) and a 2.90% medicare tax. For 1995, the 12.40% OASDI tax is applied against the first $61,200 of self-employment income. The 2.90% medicare portion is applied against all self-employment income. Table 4.8 summarizes the calculation of FICA taxes.

Table 4.8 *1995 FICA Taxes*

A	B	C	D	E	F
Total FICA Tax Individual 7.65%	**Social Security Portion 6.20%**	**Medicare Portion 1.45%**	**Total FICA Tax Self-Employed 15.30%**	**Social Security Portion 12.40%**	**Medicare Portion 2.90%**
Maximum Taxable Wages	$61,200	Unlimited	Maximum Taxable Income	$61,200	Unlimited

State and Local Income Taxes

The third and fourth types of income taxes, respectively, are state and local income taxes. With each change in the level of government, there is a change in the methodology used to calculate the tax. Each state calculates the state income tax due according to its own tax return form, and each state differs. Some states have no state income tax (Washington and Wyoming), some have a flat income tax rate—that is, one tax bracket exists (Illinois and Indiana)—and some (the majority) have progressive income tax rates.

Depending on where you live and work, you may be subject to a variety of local taxes such as county, municipal, township, school district, and special district taxes. Over 83,000 local governments existed as of the last Census of Governments. This is an enormous number, compared to the 50 state governments (not including the District of Columbia) and the federal government. Local governments also vary in the type of income taxes levied, their rate structure, and the formula for calculating any tax due.

Now that we have finished discussing income taxes—the first category of taxes in Table 4.1—let's move on to the remaining categories of taxes: sales taxes, license taxes, property taxes, and transfer taxes.

Sales, License, Property, and Transfer Taxes

Sales taxes vary from state to state, but they are basically taxes levied on purchased items, both durable and nondurable products. We also include excise taxes in this category. An excise tax is defined as "a tax or duty levied on the manufacture, sale, or consumption of certain commodities." In simple terms, excise taxes are the equivalent of a sales tax placed on items such as alcohol and tobacco, and they include manufacturers' excise taxes (for firearms, shells, cartridges, pistols, revolvers, bows and arrows) and miscellaneous excise taxes.

License taxes, the third category of taxes, include taxes for motor vehicles and their operation (taxes to operate a private or commercial vehicle), corporation licensing (franchise license taxes), alcoholic beverages (for manufacturing, importing and wholesaling), amusements (race tracks, theaters, athletic events, and pool halls), running certain types of businesses, hunting and fishing, and other licenses (marriage licenses, for example). These taxes are applied according to the laws of each state.

Property taxes, the fourth category of taxes, are taxes paid on real and personal property and tangible and intangible property. Real property (a personal residence, for instance) and personal property (for example, stocks and bonds) are taxed according to the laws of each state.

The fifth and final category is transfer taxes. They are taxes on gifts (for example, a home, stocks, or bonds) paid by the giver of the gift and taxes on the value of an individual's estate (the total value of an individual's assets) at death. Typically, gift taxes and estate taxes are paid out of savings since they are not usually part of an individual's budget.

Since you will most likely be faced with paying income taxes, sales taxes, license taxes, property taxes, and transfer taxes during your lifetime, it is important to understand how each one may affect various stages of your financial planning process.

Recap: You have just learned the basic concepts of taxation. For those of you who are learning them for the first time, be patient. If the text seems difficult, don't get discouraged. It will get easier as the big financial planning picture unfolds. If you are uncertain about a portion of the information we've presented, reread that section of the text…and refer back to it as often as necessary for you to feel confident that you understand the concepts and methods we're presenting. You will be dealing with taxes for the rest of your working lifetime and in retirement. The goal of this financial planning system is to put you in the driver's seat. To do that, you must be comfortable with and learn to use what we are teaching.

Table 4.9 *The Expanded Five-Step Economic Model*

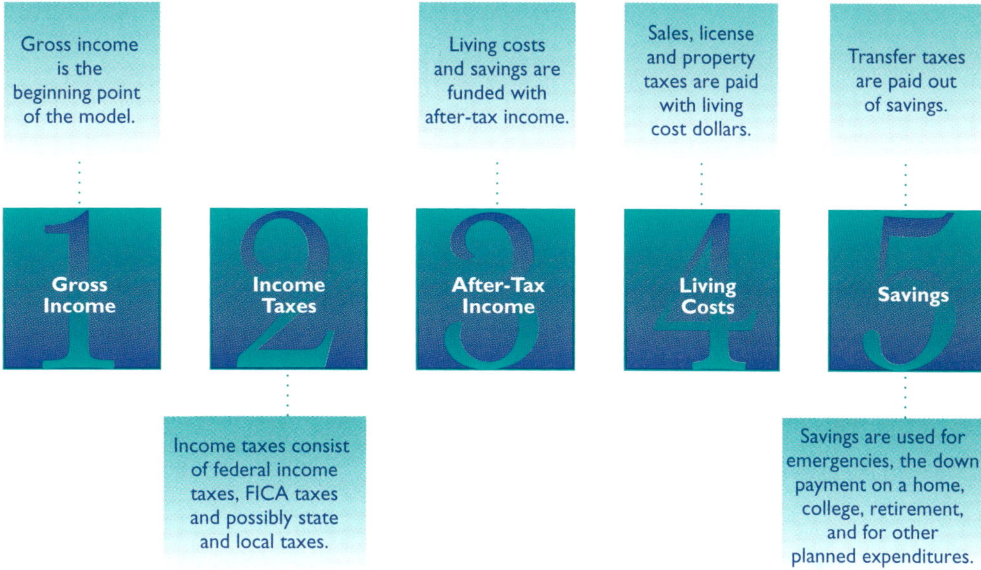

Table 4.9 shows how what you have just learned about taxes fits into the five-step economic model. In fact, all of the modules in our learning system for financial planning are interconnected and tie into this five-step economic model.

We will refer to it frequently throughout the book. This enables us to reinforce and expand upon the most important financial planning concepts in each module as we build upon your base of knowledge.

Module 5 The Five-Step Economic Model

Although we have referred to "The Five-Step Economic Model" before, Module 5 examines it in more depth. In the beginning portion of this module we will explain the reasoning behind the need for this model. We will then explain how the model is actually used when preparing a financial plan.

The Need for the Five-Step Economic Model

At the end of Module 3 we discussed how determining living costs varies from person to person and involves a four-step process. Let's review those steps. They are (1) identifying your current stage in the life cycle (single, married with or without children, single parent, or retired individual), (2) determining your standard of living, (3) accounting for independent changes in living costs that could occur from year to year, and (4) increasing your living costs by the rate of inflation.

Table 5.1 shows that regardless of your stage in the life cycle, your gross income must increase annually to keep pace with increases in your living costs as measured by inflation.

Table 5.1 *The Five-Step Economic Model*

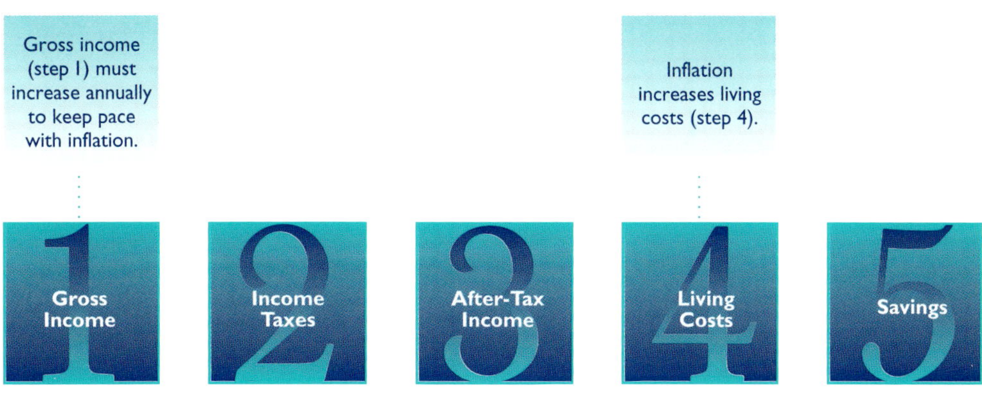

Regardless of the extent to which inflation affects your personal financial plan, it generally requires that your income increase annually to maintain *the same standard of living*. Although your gross income must increase annually to keep pace with inflation, technically speaking it is not gross income (step 1) that you use to pay for living costs, but after-tax income (step 3). As a result, not only must your gross income increase annually to keep pace with inflation, but also—and more importantly—your after-tax income must increase. This brings up two important questions that you should ask:

(1) Is my gross income keeping pace with inflation annually in percentage terms, as measured by the Consumer Price Index (CPI) ?

(2) If my gross income is keeping pace with inflation, is my after-tax income also keeping pace?

If your after-tax income is *not* increasing at the rate required to keep pace with inflation, there can be only two reasons:

(1) The percentage increase in your gross income is *not* keeping pace with the percentage increase in inflation, as measured by the CPI; or

(2) The percentage increase in your gross income is keeping pace—perhaps even exceeding the percentage increase in inflation—but this increase is offset by a rise in income tax rates.

While the first reason is easy to see, the second may take a little more thought. To truly understand how income taxes can prevent percentage increases in gross income from *flowing through* to after-tax income demands a thorough understanding of the five-step economic model.

The Flow-Through Concept Defined

In simple terms, the flow-through concept states that in order to maintain the same standard of living, the annual percentage increases in gross income that are needed to keep pace with inflation must *flow through* from your gross income to your after-tax income. For example, if the inflation rate is 4% in the current year, then your gross income and after-tax income should increase by at least 4%, assuming that your entire budget for living costs increases with inflation. If your after-tax income does not increase in this manner, then your standard of living could begin to decline, your savings rate could begin to decline, or both. Table 5.2 illustrates this concept.

Table 5.2 *The Flow-Through Concept*

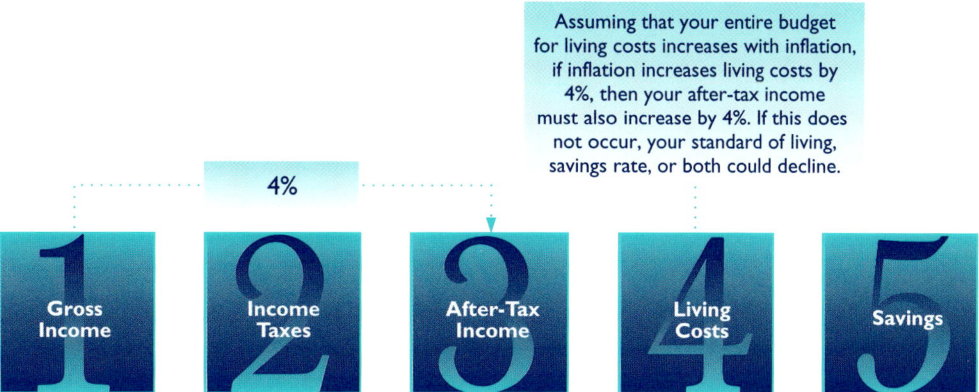

Income Taxes

As we discussed in Module 4, income taxes consist primarily of federal income tax and FICA tax. A third type of income tax is state income tax, which is levied in some—but not all—states. A fourth type is local income tax, which is also levied in some—but not all—localities.

A tax rate increase in any one of the categories of income taxes will affect the percentage increase flowing through from gross income to after-tax income. To help you see how increasing income tax rates can hinder percentage increases in gross income from flowing through to after-tax income, let's take a look at income tax rate structures.

Income Tax Rate Structures

Generally speaking, there are only three types of tax rate structures in an income tax system: (1) a proportionate income tax rate structure, (2) a progressive income tax rate structure, and (3) a regressive income tax rate structure (see Table 5.3). Let's briefly examine each one.

Table 5.3 *The Three Types of Income Tax Rate Structures*

1	2	3
Proportionate	**Progressive**	**Regressive**
Percentage tax rate applied is constant	Percentage tax rate applied increases	Percentage tax rate applied decreases

A proportionate income tax rate structure is one in which the tax rate (in percentage terms) remains constant as taxable income increases. An example is certain state income tax rate structures where one flat rate is applied to all taxable income. In Pennsylvania, for instance, the state income tax was a flat 2.8% for 1995, which was applied against all taxable income, regardless of the amount.

A progressive income tax rate structure is one where the tax rate (in percentage terms) increases as taxable income increases. A good example is the federal income tax rate structure, which increases the tax rate for taxable income after each threshold amount (see Module 4).

A regressive income tax rate structure is one in which the tax rate (in percentage terms) decreases as taxable income increases. For example, if the first $15,000 of taxable income is taxed at a 15% rate and the rate decreases to 12% on taxable income thereafter, this is a regressive tax rate.

The social security portion of FICA taxes operates as a regressive tax. This is because, as we explained in Module 4, a tax rate of 6.2% (12.4% for self-employed individuals) is applied to the first $61,200 (ceiling amount) of taxable wages for 1995. All taxable wages thereafter—think of such wages as a second bracket—have a tax rate of 0%. Therefore, as your taxable wages increase beyond the ceiling amount, the social security tax you pay as a percentage of taxable wages decreases (regresses). (Note that the medicare portion of FICA taxes has no ceiling amount and is therefore a proportionate—constant rate—tax.)

Here is the crucial point: When tax rates within a given tax rate structure do not fluctuate from year to year, *only proportionate (constant) or regressive (decreasing) income tax rates* allow percentage increases in your gross income to flow through *intact* to after-tax income. If tax rates increase (regardless of whether the tax rate structure is proportionate, progressive, or regressive), then some—if not all—of the percentage increase in your gross income will be offset by the tax rate increase. In turn, this reduces the percentage amount of gross income that flows through to your after-tax income. An increase in tax rate affects the amount of flow-through to your after-tax income regardless of whether the increase in gross income is less than, equal to, or greater than the inflation rate for that year.

Now let's consider the various types of income taxes and their respective tax rate structures. We'll begin with the federal income tax and explain how, despite it being a progressive tax, the rates are adjusted annually for inflation using a procedure called indexing.

Indexing

Because inflation is a chronic problem that usually requires increases in gross income each year to maintain the same standard of living, the federal government began indexing the federal tax system in 1989. What indexing means is that adjustments are made each year to the federal standard deduction amount, the federal personal exemption amount, and the federal tax rate tables to counter the effects of inflation. These annual adjustments are made because the federal government is aware that taxpayers should not be required to move into a higher tax bracket and pay a higher income tax rate if their incomes are increasing annually at a rate *no higher than the rate of inflation.*

As an example, if inflation for the current year is 4%, then after-tax income must also increase by 4% to maintain the same standard of living. This assumes that living costs all increase with inflation. The only way that the 4% increase in gross income can flow through to after-tax income is for the percentage tax rate (speaking here only of federal income tax) to remain constant. If the tax rate increases, then some or all of the increase in gross income *will not flow through to your after-tax income.*

The federal government indexes the federal tax system by *increasing* the standard deduction and personal exemption amounts each year (both reduce taxable income) and by raising the threshold amounts in the tax brackets. Keep in mind that the threshold amounts represent the maximum *taxable income* level in each bracket before the taxpayer moves into the next bracket and that the federal tax is calculated against taxable income.

The effect of indexing is to allow our progressive federal tax system to function on a year-to-year basis as if it were a proportionate (constant) tax system to the extent that your annual increases in taxable income do not exceed the annual rate of inflation. The annual adjustments to the standard deduction, personal exemption, and threshold amounts are calculated by the IRS using a formula based on the prior year's inflation rate.

Table 5.4 *The Indexing Process*

A	B	C	D
Year	Standard Deduction Amount	Personal Exemption Amount	Threshold Amount 15% Bracket
1991	$5,700	$2,150	$34,000
1992	6,000	2,300	35,800
1993	6,200	2,350	36,900
1994	6,350	2,450	38,000
1995	6,550	2,500	39,000

In Table 5.4, the standard deduction amounts, personal exemption amounts, and threshold amounts are indicated in columns B, C, and D for the years 1991-1995. The threshold amounts in column D are for a married couple filing a joint return in the 15% tax bracket. These threshold figures indicate the taxable income amount at which a taxpayer moves from a 15% marginal tax rate to a 28% marginal tax rate.

The most important concept to understand in Table 5.4 is that the standard deduction, personal exemption, and threshold amounts all *increase* each year (assuming the CPI reading is inflationary). Based on these annual adjustments, theoretically speaking, if you are presently in a 15% federal tax bracket, you can stay in that bracket forever assuming that your taxable income does not increase more than inflation each year.

In summary, then, remember that the standard deduction and personal exemption amounts are used to reduce the amount of *taxable income*. Raising these amounts yearly helps to offset annual increases in taxpayers' taxable income. Combining the increases in the standard deduction and personal exemption amounts with increases in the threshold amounts makes it possible for you to remain in the same tax bracket even as your taxable income increases annually.

Staying in the same tax bracket means that the *same tax rate* is applied to your taxable income each year–in effect, allowing your federal income tax rate to remain proportionate (constant). By doing so, this allows the percentage increase in your gross income to flow through to your after-tax income.

Consider what would happen if the federal tax system were not indexed: If your federal taxable income was $39,000 in 1995 but the threshold amount for the 15% bracket remained at $38,000 (unchanged from 1994), the last $1,000 of your taxable income would be taxed at 28%, as opposed to 15%. This would increase your income tax by $130 ($280 versus $150).

FICA, State and Local Taxes

Now let's examine FICA, state, and local taxes. FICA taxes are not indexed but are a proportionate (constant) tax. Keep in mind that even though the percentage tax rate is constant, the total dollar amount of your tax due will still increase as your taxable income (taxable wages) increases. Therefore, proportionate FICA tax rates allow for percentage increases in gross income to flow through to after-tax income as long as the FICA tax rate remains at its current level from year-to-year.

It is appropriate here to reemphasize a point mentioned earlier regarding FICA taxes. Although FICA taxes are proportionate, there is a maximum cut-off point–ceiling amount–after which the social security portion of FICA tax is not applied. At that point, the social security portion of FICA taxes actually becomes regressive–that is, the tax rate decreases to 0%. The ceiling amount increases each year based on the rate of inflation. For example, the ceiling amounts were $57,600 in 1993, $60,600 in 1994, and $61,200 in 1995.

Some state income taxes are partially indexed, while local taxes typically are not. The indexing of each state's income tax system has to do with its relationship to the federal tax system. The starting point for the calculation of state taxes in many instances is federal taxable income or federal adjusted gross income (AGI).

To the extent that federal taxable income is the starting point, state taxable income shares in the adjustments made to the standard deduction amount and the personal exemption amount. If federal AGI is the starting point for the preparation of your state income tax return, then the adjustments to the standard deduction amount and the personal exemption amount have no effect because they are deductions from adjusted gross income. Adjustments to the federal tax tables, which are part of the federal indexing process, have no relational effect on the state income tax system.

Typically, local income taxes are not adjusted (indexed) for inflation. However, the extent to which they are proportionate dictates how much of your increase in gross income will flow through to after-tax income.

We will now put numbers into the five-step economic model to begin showing you how the model applies to your financial planning process.

Table 5.5 *The Five-Step Economic Model*

Year	Step 1 Gross Income	Step 2 Income Taxes	Step 3 After-Tax Income	Step 4 Living Costs	Step 5 Savings
1995	$40,000	$8,848	$31,152	$26,479	$4,673

Table 5.5 illustrates the five-step economic model for a married U.S. household (husband and wife with no children). Our married couple has combined gross earned income of $40,000 in 1995 (step 1), which is subject to federal, FICA, state, and local income taxes. Income taxes for our married couple total $8,848 (step 2). Remember that FICA taxes are levied against gross earned income while other federal, state, and local income taxes are applied against various forms of income as designated on the tax return forms.

The couple's after-tax income is $31,152 (step 3), which is gross income minus income taxes. Assuming that the couple saves 15% of their after-tax income (step 5), living costs (step 4) are $26,479. Also assume that the $26,479 of living costs includes expense items in the seven product groups of the CPI, which were described in Module 3. To review, these product groups are as follows: food and beverages, housing, apparel and upkeep, transportation, medical care, entertainment and other goods and services. Savings (step 5) equals $4,673 (step 3 minus step 4).

Table 5.6 *1995 Income Taxes*

A	B	C	D	E	F
1995 Income Taxes	**Gross Income**	**Deductions**	**Taxable Income**	**Tax Rate**	**Tax**
Federal Taxes	$40,000	$11,550*	$28,450	15.00%	$4,268
FICA Taxes	$40,000	Not Applicable	$40,000	7.65%	$3,060
State Taxes	$40,000	$0	$40,000	2.80%	$1,120
Local Taxes	$40,000	$0	$40,000	1.00%	$ 400
Total Income Taxes					**$8,848**

Note: State and local taxes are not levied in every state; however, they are used in this example.
**Standard deduction of $6,550 plus two personal exemptions totalling $5,000 ($2,500 per exemption).*

Table 5.6 shows how our married couple's total income tax amount of $8,848 was calculated. The $4,268 federal tax on $40,000 of gross income was determined as follows:

(1) The 1995 standard deduction of $6,550 for a married couple filing a joint return was subtracted from the couple's gross income of $40,000.

(2) The $5,000 personal exemptions (two dependents times the 1995 personal exemption of $2,500) was subtracted. This results in $28,450 of taxable income (column D).

(3) According to the 1995 tax rate schedules for a married couple filing a joint return with taxable income of $28,450, the tax rate was 15% (column E). Multiplying $28,450 by 15% yields a federal tax liability of $4,268 (column F). We are using the tax rate from the appropriate tax rate schedule in Table 5.6 to show you how the tax was calculated in this example. In practice, however, the federal tax would not be computed by using the tax rate schedule (applying a 15% tax rate to $28,450), but rather by using the *tax rate tables* (which indicates a federal income tax of $4,264). Using the tax rate tables is the correct procedure because taxable income ($28,450) is less than $100,000. Remember, as we mentioned earlier, the tax rate tables are used for taxable income less than $100,000; the tax rate schedules are used for taxable income of $100,000 and above.

(4) Moving on to the remaining taxes in Table 5.6, we see that FICA taxes–7.65% of gross earnings–are $3,060 (column F).

(5) State taxes of $1,120 are 2.80% of taxable income, and local taxes of $400 are 1% of taxable income (column F). Note that gross income and taxable income are the same ($40,000) for both state and local taxes because it is assumed that there are no available deductions or exemptions.

(6) The total of all income taxes due is $8,848 (bottom of column F).

Dollar and Percentage Amounts

Using the five-step economic model enables us to determine two primary pieces of information: first, how gross income in *dollar amounts* is allocated among income taxes, after-tax income, living costs, and savings; and second, the percentage amounts that income taxes, after-tax income, living costs, and savings represent within the model. Table 5.7 presents the dollar and percentage amounts for our married household with no children.

Table 5.7 *Dollar and Percentage Amount Calculations*

$40,000	–	**$8,848**	=	**$31,152**	–	**$26,479**	=	**$4,673**
100%		**22%**		**78%**				
		$ Amount in Step 2 ÷ $ Amount in Step 1		$ Amount in Step 3 ÷ $ Amount in Step 1		▼		▼
				$31,152	–	**$26,479**	=	**$4,673**
				100%		**85%**		**15%**
						$ Amount in Step 4 ÷ $ Amount in Step 3		$ Amount in Step 5 ÷ $ Amount in Step 3

It is important to understand that gross income minus income taxes always equals after-tax income and that after-tax income minus living costs always equals money available for savings. The percentage calculations of income taxes (step 2) and after-tax income (step 3), as a standard rule, will always be expressed as a percentage of gross income (step 1), and the percentage calculations of living costs (step 4) and savings (step 5) will always be expressed as a percentage of after-tax income (step 3). Thus in Table 5.7, income taxes are 22% of gross income ($8,848 ÷ $40,000 = 22%), and after-tax income is 78% of gross income ($31,152 ÷ $40,000 = 78%).

Continuing with our example, living costs are 85% of after-tax income ($26,479 ÷ $31,152 = 85%). Savings represent 15% of after-tax income ($4,673 ÷ $31,152 = 15%).

In this example, our *savings rate* is 15%. As you recall, 15% is the minimum recommended savings rate in our financial planning system.

Appendix C contains the savings rates for the country as a whole, during the period 1949–1994. During this forty-six year period, savings rates were single-digit ranging from a low of 3.7% in 1949 to a high of 9% in 1973. The minimum 15% savings rate we recommend is given only as a benchmark. The savings rate needed to achieve the various goals of an individual's or family's financial plan can only be determined based on their specific needs, time frames and the after-tax rates of return achieved when investing. The concepts surrounding these topics will be addressed in Module 9.

Summary of Dollar and Percentage Amounts

It is essential that you understand the mechanics of the five-step economic model as shown in Table 5.7. This is not theory. It is the *foundation* on which any successful long-term financial plan is built. Think about it. If you were asked how much of your gross income goes to income taxes each year and how much flows through to after-tax income, would you know? Furthermore, would you know how much of your after-tax income you spend on living costs and how much you save? To establish a financial plan you must know the dollar and percentage allocations of gross income to income taxes and after-tax income and the dollar and percentage allocations of after-tax income to living costs and savings.

We'll now use the five-step economic model in three different scenarios to enhance your understanding of these principles. Our first example illustrates income that keeps pace with projected inflation. Our second example illustrates income increasing at a greater rate than projected inflation. Finally, our third example illustrates income increasing at a lesser rate than projected inflation.

The goal in the first scenario is to maintain the same standard of living and savings rate each year. The goal in the second scenario is to improve the standard of living, increase the savings rate, or both. In the third scenario, the goal is to live within one's means. Note: These three approaches are guidelines – not exact procedures – for establishing a financial plan.

Let's now examine our first scenario – after-tax income keeping pace with inflation.

Table 5.8 *After-Tax Income Keeping Pace with Inflation*

	Step 1	Step 2	Step 3	Step 4	Step 5
Year	Gross Income	Income Taxes	After-Tax Income	Living Costs	Savings
1995	$40,000	$8,848	$31,152	$26,479	$4,673
	x 1.04 =	x 1.04 =	x 1.04 =	Variable Costs x 1.04 + Fixed Costs =	Step 3 – Step 4
1996	$41,600	$9,202	$32,398	$27,196	$5,202
Increase	4%	4%	4%	3%	11%

Table 5.8 shows the 1995 dollar amounts for our married household with no children. In this example, we'll assume that the year 1995 has just ended and project that inflation for 1996 will be 4%. The 4% increase used in the model represents the growth rate. The growth rate is a percentage rate that can be less than, equal to, or greater than the projected rate of inflation.

For 1996 after-tax income to keep pace with the projected 4% rate of inflation, we must increase 1995 gross income, income taxes, and after-tax income by 4%. The 4% increase will then be applied only against the 1995 living costs that are variable to arrive at the projected 1996 living cost figures. Obviously, any items that are fixed in amount remain the same in 1996.

Our couple has three living cost items that are fixed in amount: the mortgage, a car loan, and a credit card payment. Obviously, if a fixed payment, such as a car loan, was going to be paid off in the upcoming year, only the balance that remained on the car loan (and *not* a full year's worth of payments) would be included in that component of total living costs. Savings are the difference between steps 3 and 4.

Returning to our example: To arrive at this couple's 1996 gross income, income taxes, after-tax income, and variable living costs, we multiply the 1995 figures by 1.04–the conversion factor. That factor is determined using the conversion formula–that is, by dividing the annual inflation rate (4% in our example) by 100 and then adding 1 (4 ÷ 100 + 1= 1.04). (Refer back to Module 2 if you'd like to refresh your memory regarding the conversion formula.)

Multiplying the 1995 amounts by 1.04–which sets up the flow-through process from gross income to after-tax income–gives us our couple's 1996 projected amounts. Note that the 4% increase in gross income flows through to after-tax income because income taxes remain a constant percentage, even though they increase in dollar amount (1996 income taxes of $9,202 are 22.12% of 1996 gross income of $41,600, which is the same percentage rate as in 1995). Table 5.9 shows the 4% increase in variable living costs that is used to arrive at the 1996 amounts. The 1996 fixed amounts remain the same as in 1995.

Table 5.9 *Projecting Living Costs*

	1995 Actual Living Costs	× 1.04 =	1996 Projected Living Costs
Food and Beverages			
Food	$ 4,501		$ 4,681
Housing			
Mortgage	$ 6,046	Fixed Payment	$ 6,046
Real Estate Taxes	2,800		2,912
Utilities/Household Expenses	1,850		1,924
Homeowner's Insurance	725		754
Subtotal	$ 11,421		$ 11,636
Apparel and Upkeep	$ 1,589		$ 1,653
Clothing			
Transportation			
Auto Loan Payments	$ 2,450	Fixed Payment	$ 2,450
Car Insurance	875		910
Gasoline and Repairs	901		937
Public Transportation	275		286
Subtotal	$ 4,501		$ 4,583
Medical Care			
Medical Costs/Insurance	$ 1,194		$ 1,242
Dental/Eye Examinations	475		494
Prescription Drugs	185		192
Subtotal	$ 1,854		$ 1,928
Entertainment			
Vacations	$ 559		$ 581
Fitness Programs	375		390
Video Rentals	125		130
Subtotal	$ 1,059		$ 1,101
Other Goods and Services			
Life Insurance	$ 500		$ 520
Credit Card Debt	50	Fixed Payment	50
Charitable Giving	125		130
Personal Care Items	879		914
Subtotal	$ 1,554		$ 1,614
Total Living Costs	**$26,479**		**$27,196**

Fixed payments, noted in the table, are not affected by inflation. (Note: Credit card payments can decrease over time as principal is reduced.)

According to Table 5.9, our couple's projected living costs for 1996 are $27,196. Subtracting this amount from the couple's projected 1996 after-tax income of $32,398 (See Table 5.8) leaves them with projected savings of $5,202. Since not all living costs increase with inflation, the couple's projected savings increased 11% (which is more than the projected 4% inflation rate).

This concept of increasing gross income, income taxes and after-tax income by the projected inflation rate, but applying that rate against only the *variable* living cost components allows you to adjust appropriately for inflation. By using this approach, projected savings may increase by more than the projected rate of inflation (depending, of course, on the portion of living costs that are fixed).

Now let's examine after-tax income outpacing inflation.

Table 5.10 *After-Tax Income Outpacing Inflation*

	Step 1	Step 2	Step 3	Step 4	Step 5
Year	Gross Income	Income Taxes	After-Tax Income	Living Costs	Savings
1995	$40,000	$8,848	$31,152	$26,479	$4,673
	x 1.06 =	x 1.06 =	x 1.06 =	Variable Costs x 1.04 + Fixed Costs =	Step 3 – Step 4
1996	$42,400	$9,379	$33,021	$27,196	$5,825
Increase	6%	6%	6%	3%	25%

In Table 5.10, the 1995 dollar amounts for our married household with no children are the same as in Table 5.8, and inflation for 1996 is also projected to be 4%. Again, living costs, excluding the fixed mortgage, auto loan, and credit card payment, are variable, but this scenario assumes that the couple is able to outpace inflation because their income is increasing at a 6% growth rate–2% *above* the projected rate of inflation. In economic terms, when income is increasing at a greater percentage than inflation, the excess over the rate of inflation is a *real increase*. In our example, the projected real increase is 2%. (Note that because the fixed living cost components don't increase with inflation, the real increase is actually greater.)

Therefore, 1995 gross income, income tax, and after-tax income amounts are multiplied by 1.06, but the variable living cost components will increase by only 4% (using 1.04 as the conversion factor). The 1995 fixed costs are then added to the 1996 inflation-adjusted costs. Savings is determined by taking the difference between steps 3 and 4. Again, remember that the projected 6% increase in gross income flows through to after-tax income because income taxes again remain a constant percentage although they increase in dollar amount. As a result, our couple experiences a real increase in after-tax income, which will augment savings by 25%–from $4,673 in 1995 to $5,825 in 1996. If the real increase in after-tax income is not used to increase savings, it could be used to improve their standard of living (by spending more money on living costs than is necessary to keep pace with inflation).

Now let's look at our third scenario: after-tax income lagging behind inflation.

Table 5.11 *After-Tax Income Lagging Behind Inflation*

	Step 1	Step 2	Step 3	Step 4	Step 5
Year	**Gross Income**	**Income Taxes**	**After-Tax Income**	**Living Costs**	**Savings**
1995	**$40,000**	**$8,848**	**$31,152**	**$26,479**	**$4,673**
	x 1.02 =	x 1.02 =	x 1.02 =	Variable Costs x 1.06 + Fixed Costs =	Step 3 – Step 4
1996	**$40,800**	**$9,025**	**$31,775**	**$27,559**	**$4,216**
Increase	2%	2%	2%	4%	-10%

Table 5.11 also has the same 1995 dollar amounts for our married household with no children. In this example, however, we will assume that the inflation rate will be 6% but income will increase at only 2%, 4% *below* the projected rate of inflation.

As in Tables 5.8 and 5.10, we will again assume that, except for the fixed mortgage, auto loan, and credit card payment, living costs are variable. When income increases at a lesser percentage rate than inflation, the deficiency is called a *real decrease*. In our case, the projected real decrease is 4%. (Keep in mind that because only variable living costs increase with inflation and our budget also contains fixed components, the real decrease will actually be less.)

In Table 5.11, therefore, we will increase our couple's 1995 gross income, income tax, and after-tax income amounts by 2% (a conversion factor of 1.02). However, we will increase the variable living cost components by 6% (a conversion factor of 1.06). Then we'll add the 1995 fixed costs to the 1996 inflation-adjusted costs and subtract the dollar amount in step 4 from the dollar amount in step 3 to determine the couple's savings. The 2% increase in gross income flows through to after-tax income because income taxes remain a constant percentage. The 6% increase in the variable living cost components (due to a 6% inflation rate) will result in an overall increase to living costs of only 4%. As a result, a real decrease will occur that will reduce the couple's savings by 10%–from $4,673 to $4,216.

One final point: In establishing our couple's financial plan, the projected increase to living costs (step 4) could have been forecast to be less than the projected rate of inflation. A lesser rate could have been projected if our couple believed that they would be able to contain costs by controlling their expenses–for example, staying away from certain food groups that are increasing in price, shopping at discount outlets, lowering their standard of living, or simply putting some expenditures on hold.

Now you are beginning to see some of the possibilities of this financial planning system. We've laid the groundwork. In Module 6, "Designing Your Personal Financial Plan," you will use an expanded version of the five-step economic model to design your own financial plan, following one of the three scenarios we've just explained: keeping pace with projected inflation, outpacing projected inflation, or falling behind projected inflation.

Designing Your Personal Financial Plan

Module 6 introduces an expanded version of the five-step economic model to design, implement and monitor your own personal financial plan. Let's quickly review the model shown in Table 6.1.

Table 6.1 *The Five-Step Economic Model*

Introduced in Module 3, the five-step economic model is the foundation for our financial planning system. Using this model allows you to carefully monitor how your gross income (step 1) is allocated among income taxes (step 2), after-tax income (step 3), living costs (step 4), and savings (step 5).

Establishing Goals

To properly manage a financial plan over long periods of time, you must first establish your goals for each step of the five-step economic model. Then you must compare your actual results to these goals, which will immediately point out any differences.

Therefore, as we continue to work with the five-step economic model, we will be comparing your actual amounts to target amounts (your desired goals). This will allow you to determine if differences between actual and target amounts are occurring on a year-to-year basis and whether you are meeting (and perhaps even exceeding) your goals. Table 6.2 illustrates the concept of comparing actual to target amounts for each step of the five-step economic model.

Table 6.2 *Actual Minus Target Amounts*

Step 1			Step 2			Step 3		
Actual Gross Income	Target Gross Income	Actual Minus Target	Actual Income Taxes	Target Income Taxes	Actual Minus Target	Actual After-Tax Income	Target After-Tax Income	Actual Minus Target

Step 4			Step 5		
Actual Living Costs	Target Living Costs	Actual Minus Target	Actual Savings	Target Savings	Actual Minus Target

The Five-Step Economic Model Profile

Now let's take a look at the five-step economic model profile, which is simply an expansion of Table 6.2. Think of the five-step economic model profile as a *financial planning road map*. Its ultimate purpose is to allow you to establish guidelines for maintaining or improving your standard of living, taking inflation into account, while at the same time meeting your savings goals. The profile enables you to accomplish this by establishing target amounts for gross income, income taxes, after-tax income, living costs, and savings based on a growth rate that is less than, equal to, or greater than the projected rate of inflation. Table 6.3 shows a five-year version of the five-step economic model profile.

Table 6.3 *The Five-Year, Five-Step Economic Model Profile*

	Step 1			Step 2			Step 3		
Year	Actual Gross Income	Target Gross Income	Actual Minus Target	Actual Income Taxes	Target Income Taxes	Actual Minus Target	Actual After-Tax Income	Target After-Tax Income	Actual Minus Target
Base									
1									
2									
3									
4									
5									
Total									

	Step 4			Step 5		
Year	Actual Living Costs	Target Living Costs	Actual Minus Target	Actual Savings	Target Savings	Actual Minus Target
Base						
1						
2						
3						
4						
5						
Total						

Setting Up Your Five-Year, Five-Step Economic Model Profile

We will now illustrate how to develop your own five-year, five-step economic model profile, assuming the year 1995 has just ended and we are projecting annual target amounts for each year from 1996 through 2000. (As a rule, we recommend that you develop projections for five-year periods). For purposes of this example, we'll refer to the information for 1995 for our married household with no children presented in Module 5. Their combined gross earned income is $40,000; aggregate federal, FICA, state, and local income taxes are $8,848; after-tax income is $31,152; living costs are $26,479; and savings are $4,673.

Because the purpose of the profile is to determine target amounts for gross income, income taxes, after-tax income, living costs, and savings, we must start with beginning base amounts. These beginning base amounts are not arbitrary numbers but are the actual amounts (in each of the five steps of the economic model) for the year prior to the beginning year of the profile (called the base year–1995 in our example).

The next step is to project target amounts for each step of the profile. Although in Module 5 we discussed projecting amounts that keep pace, outpace and lag behind inflation, in this module we will illustrate using the profile only for amounts that keep pace with inflation. Once you see how simply the profile works in this scenario, you will be able to adapt it to any type of economic situation you wish to project.

Projecting Target Amounts

Let's assume that the annual rate of inflation is expected to be 2.5% during the five-year period from 1996 to 2000. To increase the base year's target amounts by this projected inflation rate, we need to use the conversion formula to change the annual rate of inflation into a conversion factor, as shown in the following equation:

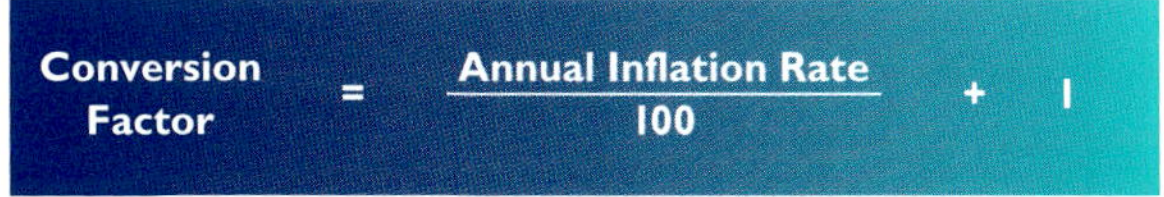

$$\text{Conversion Factor} = \frac{\text{Annual Inflation Rate}}{100} + 1$$

Changing the annual rate of inflation into a conversion factor (as we illustrated in Module 5) is necessary to calculate the effect of compounding inflation. In our example, dividing our projected inflation rate of 2.5% by 100 and adding 1 equals 1.025–the conversion factor. (Note: If there is no inflation, your amounts will remain constant from the prior year to the current year. If there is deflation, the conversion factor will be less than 1.)

Table 6.4 inserts the base amounts into the five-step economic model profile. We recommend that you use a calculator, if you have one, to follow the calculations.

Table 6.4 *The Five-Year, Five-Step Economic Model Profile*

	Step 1			Step 2			Step 3		
Year	Actual Gross Income	Target Gross Income	Actual Minus Target	Actual Income Taxes	Target Income Taxes	Actual Minus Target	Actual After-Tax Income	Target After-Tax Income	Actual Minus Target
1995	$40,000			$8,848			$31,152		
1996		x 1.025 = $41,000			x 1.025 = $9,069			x 1.025 = $31,931	
1997		x 1.025 = $42,025			x 1.025 = $9,296			x 1.025 = $32,729	
1998		x 1.025 = $43,076			x 1.025 = $9,528			x 1.025 = $33,547	
1999		x 1.025 = $44,153			x 1.025 = $9,767			x 1.025 = $34,386	
2000		x 1.025 = $45,256			x 1.025 = $10,011			x 1.025 = $35,246	

	Step 4			Step 5		
Year	Actual Living Costs	Target Living Costs	Actual Minus Target	Actual Savings	Target Savings	Actual Minus Target
1995	$26,479			$4,673		
1996	Variable Costs*	x 1.025 + Fixed Costs = $26,929		Step 3 minus Step 4	($31,931 – $26,929) $5,002	
1997		Variable Costs x 1.025 + Fixed Costs = $27,389			($32,729 – $27,389) $5,340	
1998		Variable Costs x 1.025 + Fixed Costs = $27,860			($33,547 – $27,860) $5,687	
1999		Variable Costs x 1.025 + Fixed Costs = $28,342			($34,386 – $28,342) $6,044	
2000		Variable Costs x 1.025 + Fixed Costs = $28,835			($35,246 – $28,835) $6,411	

**Detail for target living cost figures is provided in Appendix A.*

To arrive at our annual target amounts for 1996–2000, we must increase 1995 actual gross income, income taxes and after-tax income (steps 1-3) by the projected rate of inflation. Because the actual amounts will all be increased by the same rate of inflation, the increase in target gross income flows through to target after-tax income.

This same 2.5% rate of increase is then applied to *variable* living costs. (In this example, three components are fixed in amount and therefore do not increase with inflation: a mortgage payment, an auto loan payment, and a credit card payment. These are the same 1995 living costs illustrated in Module 5.)

Applying the 2.5% rate of increase only to the variable living costs increases the 1995 $26,479 living costs to $26,929. See Appendix A for the computational detail. (Note: If all living costs were variable, the 1995 living costs would have to increase to $27,141 ($26,479 x 1.025). Savings are calculated by taking the difference between target after-tax income and target living costs.

This same procedure used to calculate the 1996 target amounts is then repeated to arrive at the target amounts for the years 1997, 1998, 1999, and 2000. Each year's target amounts become the base year amounts to which the 2.5% growth rate is applied for the following year.

Revising Target Amounts and Entering Actual Amounts

Now let's enter the actual amounts into the five-year, five-step economic model profile for the year 1996. (You'll want to update your profile using actual amounts as soon as the information is available. In our example, the actual figures for 1996 will be available sometime in early 1997, along with the 1996 actual rate of inflation.) At the beginning of each new year, there are two main sources of information you can utilize. The first will be your actual amounts for the year just ended–that is, the amounts for your actual gross income, income taxes, after-tax income, living costs, and savings. The second will be the actual rate of inflation for the year just ended. Your tax information can be compiled from your tax returns and FICA payment information. The annual rate of inflation for the year just ended is reported through financial publications, radio, and television.

Returning to our couple, let's assume that their actual amounts for 1996 are as follows: Gross income was $41,200; income taxes were $9,113; after-tax income was $32,087; living costs were $27,210; and savings were $4,877. Let's also assume that the actual rate of inflation for 1996 was 4.0%.

After we have the actual figures for gross income, income taxes, after-tax income, living costs, savings, and the actual rate of inflation for 1996, we do two things. First, we change our originally *projected* 1996 target amounts to *revised* target amounts. Second, we enter the actual amounts in our economic profile. We originally projected our 1996 target amounts using a 2.5% inflation rate. Now, at the beginning of 1997, we know that the *actual* rate of inflation for 1996 was 4%, so we need to go back and multiply the 1995 *base amounts* by a 1.04 conversion factor (representing the *actual* 4% inflation rate for 1996) instead of the 1.025 conversion factor (representing the *projected* 2.5% inflation rate).

When we originally projected target amounts, we used our best estimate of what the coming year's rate of inflation would be. Now, at the end of the year we need to compare the actual rate of inflation with the estimate we used to recalculate our target amounts if necessary. If actual inflation differed from our estimated rate of inflation, then we need to adjust our target amounts based on the objective we were attempting to reach, i.e., the objective of controlling costs when income is not keeping pace with inflation; of keeping pace with inflation; or, of outpacing inflation.

In our example, we wanted to keep pace with inflation and had originally estimated a 2.5% rate. Because the actual rate of inflation was 4%, we needed to revise our target amounts to reflect the 4% rate. Now, as a result, we are able to calculate the exact amount by which we have fallen short of our goals and include that as a portion of what we need to make up over the coming one to five years. If the actual rate of inflation had matched our estimate, no change in target amounts would have been necessary.

Table 6.5 shows the couple's actual amounts and updates the originally projected 1996 target amounts *to revised target amounts* based on the actual inflation rate of 4% versus the 2.5% we had originally projected.

Table 6.5 *Revising The Five-Year, Five-Step Economic Model Profile*

	Step 1			Step 2			Step 3		
Year	Actual Gross Income	Target Gross Income	Actual Minus Target	Actual Income Taxes	Target Income Taxes	Actual Minus Target	Actual After-Tax Income	Target After-Tax Income	Actual Minus Target
1995	$40,000			$8,848			$31,152		
	1 Actual Amount	2 Revised x 1.04 =	3 Difference	1 Actual Amount	2 Revised x 1.04 =	3 Difference	1 Actual Amount	2 Revised x 1.04 =	3 Difference
1996	$41,200	$41,600	-$400	$9,113	$9,202	-$89	$32,087	$32,398	-$311
	3.00% Increase Actual Gross Income	4.00% Actual Inflation	-1.00% Difference	3.00% Increase Actual Income Taxes	4.00% Actual Inflation	-1.00% Difference	3.00% Increase Actual After-Tax Income	4.00% Actual Inflation	-1.00% Difference

	Step 4			Step 5		
Year	Actual Living Costs	Target Living Costs	Actual Minus Target	Actual Savings	Target Savings	Actual Minus Target
1995	$26,479			$4,673		
	Variable Costs*					
	1 Actual Amount	2 Revised x 1.04 + Fixed Costs =	3 Difference	1 Actual Amount	2 Revised Step 3 – Step 4 =	3 Difference
1996	$27,210	$27,196	$14	$4,877	$5,202	-$325
	2.76% Increase Actual Living Costs	2.71% Increase Based on Actual Inflation	0.05% Difference	4.37% Increase Actual Savings	11.32% Increase Based on Actual Inflation	-6.95% Difference

**Detail for living costs is provided in Table 6.6.*

Revising the five-step economic model profile is a three-step process:

(1) The *originally* projected target amounts are changed to *revised* target amounts, if necessary, using the actual rate of inflation.

(2) The actual amounts are inserted into the profile.

(3) The revised target amounts are subtracted from the actual amounts (actual *minus* target) to determine the differences.

The percentage increases from 1995 to 1996 are shown in Table 6.5 for each step of the profile. We calculated the percentage changes for both target and actual amounts for the year by using the annual rate of return formula explained in Module 1. The percentage differences in the actual-minus-target columns were calculated by simply subtracting the target percentage from the actual percentage.

As you review the percentage changes for steps 1 through 3, note that the couple's target gross income, income taxes, and after-tax income increased by 4%, while the actual amounts for the same three steps increased by 3%. Since their entire budget is not variable, target living costs did not increase 4%, but experienced the actual increases incurred. Target and actual savings were calculated by subtracting the amounts in step 4 from those in step 3.

The differences between the couple's actual amounts and the targets set, show the extent to which the couple was, or was not, able to meet their goals for the year in each of the five steps in the model. Keep in mind that our couple's objective was to keep pace with inflation. In this example, the couple's Actual Living Costs (step 4) were higher than they had projected and their savings fell short of their targeted amount because a higher than expected inflation rate, coupled with their income not keeping pace with inflation, eroded the couple's ability to simultaneously save at their target level while maintaining their current standard of living. Vesmark's financial planning system is specifically designed to help you address these types of problems and gives you the tools to *successfully* plan for a secure financial future for you and your family.

At the beginning of each new year, after you have changed the projected target amounts to revised target amounts, inserted the actual results, and calculated the difference, you are ready to project the next five-year period. In our example, you would be projecting the next five-year period from 1997 to 2001. This would involve using your 1996 actual figures for all five steps as the base amounts and choosing a new growth rate.

Comparing Actual to Revised Target Amounts

You'll recall that our couple's goal was to keep pace with inflation. If their actual amounts of gross income, after-tax income, and savings (steps 1, 3, and 5) were to exceed their revised target amounts, it would be because their income had outpaced inflation. But, as the example of our couple clearly demonstrates, their actual amounts are less than their revised target amounts. Therefore, their income is not keeping pace with inflation. Keep in mind that this system functions in three modes: (1) controlling costs when income is not keeping pace with inflation; (2) keeping pace with inflation; or (3) outpacing inflation. So, when setting and comparing your target amounts with your actual results, you must always consider the mode in which you are operating.

Regarding income taxes and living costs, steps 2 and 4, the first point to keep in mind is that these are subtraction steps. That is, income taxes are subtracted from gross income to arrive at after-tax income, and living costs are subtracted from after-tax income to arrive at savings.

When comparing these steps, because they are subtraction steps, your thinking should be the reverse of that in comparing steps 1, 3, and 5. That means that the goal here is to have your actual amounts for income taxes and living costs be less than your target amounts. The primary reason for comparing actual to target amounts for income taxes and living costs (steps 2 and 4) is to be able to pinpoint the differences arising in after-tax income and savings (steps 3 and 5).

Steps for Using the Profile

At this point it might be helpful to review the procedures for using the five-step economic model profile. To begin, we must insert the actual base year figures for gross income, income taxes, after-tax income, living costs, and savings into the profile. (Remember, the base year is the year *prior* to the first year of the profile, and the base amounts are the *actual* amounts for that year.) The following steps explain the process for inserting the base year actual amounts.

Step 1: Base Year Actual Gross Income

In general, the actual gross income in the base year will be the total of all items of recurring gross income from Form 1040 (the U.S. individual tax return) or from the shorter forms, 1040-A or 1040 EZ (depending on which you use). *Recurring items* are items of gross income that are expected to continue in subsequent years, rather than income items that arise from a one-time event such as lottery winnings. (Note that the profile can be used for projecting single incomes or combined incomes. In our example, we are illustrating the combined incomes of a married couple with no children.)

Step 2: Base Year Actual Income Taxes

The actual total income taxes in the base year are calculated by adding actual federal, FICA, state, local, and any other income-based taxes (the existence of state and local taxes depends on the laws of each state).

Step 3: Base Year Actual After-Tax Income

Actual after-tax income in the base year is calculated by subtracting total actual income taxes from actual gross income.

Step 4: Base Year Actual Living Costs

The actual living costs in the base year are determined by adding together actual living costs.

Step 5: Base Year Actual Savings

Actual savings in the base year is the amount of actual after-tax income not spent on actual living costs (step 3 – step 4).

Living Costs

Now let's take another look at the components of the budget for living costs. Keep in mind (as we discussed in Module 3) that establishing living costs varies from person to person and involves these four steps:

(1) Identifying your stage in the life cycle (single, married with or without children, single parent, or retired individual).

(2) Establishing your standard of living (this depends on the lifestyle an individual or family desires).

(3) Accounting for independent changes in your living costs that could occur from year to year.

(4) Increasing the variable components of your living costs by the projected rate of inflation, and then adding your fixed costs.

Carefully examine your living costs in the base year. Once you are satisfied that the living cost components will be included in the following year, you should increase the variable living cost components by a projected growth rate. The fixed-cost components are then added to the inflation-adjusted variable components.

If there are any changes that would alter your living cost components, and therefore affect your savings amount in the base year, this is the point at which such changes should be made. For instance, if a household incurred large living cost expenses in a particular year because of heavy credit card spending, then this excess spending should not be projected forward. Rather, the household should attempt to lower living costs so that they are more in line with prior years before projecting target amounts.

We recommend that you construct a detailed budget for living costs using the seven product groups of the CPI (see Module 3) as a guide. Use this budget for both target and actual amounts, adding the necessary detail for the living cost components (step 4) to identify differences between actual and target amounts. Table 6.6 is an example of an actual-versus-target budget for living costs for our married couple with no children using 1995 base year actual amounts; revised 1996 target amounts calculated with the revised inflation rate of 4% instead of the projected rate of 2.5%; 1996 actual amounts; and the differences. Table 6.6 provides the detail for the actual and target living cost totals which appear in step 4 of Table 6.5.

Table 6.6 *Actual Minus Target Budget for Living Costs*

	1995 Actual Living Costs	1996 Actual Living Costs	1996 Target Living Costs (Revised at 4%)	1996 Actual Minus Target
Food and Beverages				
Food	$ 4,501	$ 4,704	$ 4,681	$ 23
Housing				
Mortgage	$ 6,046	$ 6,046	$ 6,046	$ 0
Real Estate Taxes	2,800	2,898	2,912	-14
Utilities/Household Expenses	1,850	1,915	1,924	-9
Homeowner's Insurance	725	754	754	0
Subtotal	$ 11,421	$ 11,613	$ 11,636	-$ 23
Apparel and Upkeep	$ 1,589	$ 1,661	$ 1,653	$ 8
Clothing				
Transportation				
Auto Loan Payments	$ 2,450	$ 2,450	$ 2,450	$ 0
Car Insurance	875	914	910	4
Gasoline and Repairs	901	942	937	5
Public Transportation	275	286	286	0
Subtotal	$ 4,501	$ 4,592	$ 4,583	$ 9
Medical Care				
Medical Costs/Insurance	$ 1,194	$ 1,236	$ 1,242	-$ 6
Dental/Eye Examinations	475	492	494	-2
Prescription Drugs	185	191	192	-1
Subtotal	$ 1,854	$ 1,919	$ 1,928	-$ 9
Entertainment				
Vacations	$ 559	$ 584	$ 581	$ 3
Fitness Programs	375	392	390	2
Video Rentals	125	131	130	1
Subtotal	$ 1,059	$ 1,107	$ 1,101	$ 6
Other Goods and Services				
Life Insurance	$ 500	$ 520	$ 520	$ 0
Credit Card Debt	50	50	50	0
Charitable Giving	125	130	130	0
Personal Care Items	879	914	914	0
Subtotal	$ 1,554	$ 1,614	$ 1,614	$ 0
Total Living Costs	$26,479	$27,210	$27,196	$ 14

You can construct your own budget for living costs on either a monthly or annual basis, using your checkbook register and credit card statements (our example is an annual budget). This detailed budget will enable you to make a clear analysis of your actual and target living costs.

As you examine our sample budget, note that the couple's *actual* living costs in some cases are more than, equal to, or less than the *target* amounts. Also note that their mortgage payment, auto loan payment, and credit card payment remain fixed each year.

Generally, the one variable that you can control in a financial plan is your expenses. Therefore, you should scrutinize your living costs carefully, regardless of which scenario your profile projects: keeping pace with inflation, outpacing inflation, or lagging behind inflation. Furthermore, it is up to you, as the user of our financial planning system, to determine the assumptions to make about increases in your living costs in order to arrive at your desired amount of savings.

Examining Base Amounts Each Year

Now that you know how to project target amounts, revise target amounts, enter actual amounts into the economic profile, and calculate the differences for all five steps of the profile, you know how to use this financial planning system. However, we suggest that you exercise caution before using each year's actual amounts as the *base* amounts from which to project target amounts. For instance, you might, in any given year, have an extraordinary event take place that has a dramatic impact on your actual results for that year. You could get a large raise in one year and lose your job the next year. Or your living costs could rise because of the arrival of a child, the purchase of a home, or the payment of children's college costs. When using this system, therefore, you should *not* simply plug in numbers and then multiply them by a projected growth rate; rather, you should thoroughly analyze all of the components of your financial plan.

Once you are satisfied that the base year amounts reflect what you can reasonably expect the following year, the next step is to adjust for inflation. Then, at the end of the year, change the projected target amounts to revised target amounts (if necessary), enter the actual amounts into the profile, and calculate the differences.

Projecting Ahead

In Module 9, the last module of the system, you will learn how to determine the amount of money to save to meet the following five goals of a financial plan:

(1) Establish an emergency fund;

(2) Set aside money for the down payment on a home;

(3) Meet the costs of your children's college education;

(4) Accumulate funds for your retirement; and

(5) Allocate money for planned expenditures. Once you determine how much to save, you'll then have to decide how to go about generating those savings dollars. That is where the five-step economic model profile will be a great help.

While it is easy to calculate the amount of money you need to reach a financial goal, it is difficult to actually save for that goal. Looking again at our hypothetical married couple with no children, Table 6.4 shows us how much savings the couple can accumulate during the five-year period from 1996 to 2000 if they meet the targets they set. According to our calculations in Table 6.4, our married couple's projected savings will be $28,484 ($5,002 + $5,340 + $5,687 + $6,044 + $6,411).

Advantages of the Financial Planning System

This financial planning system has several advantages:

(1) The first and most important advantage of the five-step economic model profile is that it provides a format by which you can design, implement, and monitor your complete personal financial plan in an inflationary economic environment. *The goal of this planning process is to promote savings.*

(2) This financial planning system can work for anyone at any stage of the life cycle. Moreover, the calculations necessary for using the system are easy to do. In fact, the system requires only that you be able to add, subtract, multiply, and divide. What's more, these calculations can easily be performed on a calculator.

(3) Because the five-step economic model profile contains all the information for gross income, income taxes, after-tax income, living costs, and savings, you can immediately see all the components of your financial plan. The easy-to-understand format enables you to react quickly to differences between your actual and target amounts. Furthermore, the flow of the profile tracks how your money is actually earned and spent–that is, your gross income minus income taxes equals your after-tax income, and after-tax income minus living costs equals your savings.

(4) The five-step economic model profile allows you to adjust annually for the effects of inflation (or deflation) and project the income goals and savings rates you will need to accomplish your financial goals. Many individuals are so focused on the investment aspect of a financial plan that they forget about the earnings side of the equation. If your earnings (gross income) do not keep pace with your living costs as measured by inflation, then your savings will eventually decline. If your savings decline, there will be less money to invest to reach your financial goals.

(5) The concept of comparing actual amounts to target (budgeted) amounts is the procedure corporate America uses to design its annual business plans. This same process is at work in our five-step economic model profile for financial planning.

(6) Because the profile works with both dollar and percentage amounts, you can readily determine how much additional gross income you will need to arrive at a certain after-tax income amount. For instance, if you need an additional $5,000 of after-tax income in a specific year and you know from your profile that after-tax income is 78% of your gross income, you can simply divide $5,000 by .78, which equals $6,410. This $6,410 is the amount of gross income you'll need–assuming tax rates don't change–to produce $5,000 of after-tax income. Similarly, if you want to increase savings, the model gives you all the tools you'll need to determine how to attain that goal: to increase income, lower living costs, or both.

(7) Savings, which is the goal of the five-step economic model profile, can be used to meet the primary goals of a financial plan which are:

a) To build an emergency fund;
b) To accumulate a home down payment;
c) To provide for college costs for children;
d) To save for retirement; and
e) To meet planned expenditures.

All of these will be addressed in Module 9. Once the future cost of a financial goal is determined, the amount of savings needed to reach that goal can be easily determined. (This will also be addressed in Module 9).

Note: Blank Five-Step Economic Model Profile and Living Cost Schedule forms are included in Appendix B for your convenience in designing your own personal financial plan.

Module 7 The Economy, Family Incomes and the Financial Markets

Module 7 will give you information on how the economy, family incomes, and the financial markets have fared in the post-World War II era (since 1945). We will begin by briefly touching on four topics:

(1) The causes of inflation;

(2) The expenditure equation and credit-backed demand;

(3) The business cycle; and

(4) Monetary and fiscal policy.

The first two topics will help broaden your understanding of inflation; the last two will help you relate to how the overall economy operates.

Causes of Inflation

So far in this financial planning system we have defined inflation and explained how it is measured. Now we will deal with the factors that cause inflation. The price level (the level of current prices for all types of goods and services) is the point at which the demand for goods and services meets supply. As long as the current supply and demand situation holds steady, *the price level will remain unchanged*. However, if either the demand or the supply side of the equation is altered, the imbalance that occurs will cause an increase or decrease in the price level.

As a result, there are three possible scenarios for the demand and supply equation:

(1) Demand can meet supply, resulting in a constant price level;

(2) Demand can exceed supply, causing prices to rise; and

(3) Demand can be less than supply, causing prices to fall.

Table 7.1 summarizes the three scenarios. Only scenario 2, where demand exceeds supply, theoretically causes inflation.

Table 7.1 *Demand and Supply*

1	2	3
Demand Meeting Supply Results in Steady Prices	Demand Exceeding Supply Results in Rising Prices	Demand Less Than Supply Results in Falling Prices

However, other factors can cause inflation. One is the pursuit of profitability. When businesses raise prices to increase profits within the constraints of a competitive marketplace, this causes inflation. Major wars, such as World War I (1917–1918) and World War II (1941–1945), and to a lesser extent smaller-scale wars, such as the Korean War (1950–1953), also cause inflation. During such periods, the government spends large amounts of money to finance the war effort. This spending causes prices to rise as the demand for goods and services exceeds supply. Unfortunately, after such periods, the price level typically does not recede to the levels experienced prior to the war, resulting in a sustained price level increase.

Shortages in food and energy sources also contributed to a rising price level in the post-World War II era. For example, shortages in energy occurred when the oil-producing export countries (OPEC) slowed the supply of oil. Oil shortages, in turn, meant higher gas prices at the pump. Shortages in food have taken place when drought, bad weather conditions, and other natural causes led to poor harvests. These circumstances, in turn, caused food prices to rise.

There are still other, more complex, reasons for inflation that can cause the prices of goods and services to rise. One prime example is a weak U.S. dollar. A weak dollar, by directly increasing the cost of imported goods and services, increases the price of those goods and services to U.S. consumers. Another example is import tariffs that directly increase the price of imported goods.

The Expenditure Equation and Credit-Backed Demand

Although there are various reasons accounting for inflation in the post-World War II era, the dominant one has been that demand has exceeded supply. The primary reason that the demand for goods and services has outpaced supply is *consumer borrowing*. This is because the ability to borrow has enabled the typical consumer to spend far in excess of his or her after-tax income.

You may not know that consumers account for two-thirds of the nation's spending; government and businesses account for the remaining third. In the aggregate, consumer spending comes from after-tax income (from which savings is derived) and also from money borrowed from banks or similar credit sources. While credit (borrowed money) has always supported spending in our economy, the amount of credit that consumers borrow did not begin to grow to sizable proportions until after World War II.

In the normal productive process of our economy, money is earned (gross income), and living costs are paid out of after-tax income. When the ability to borrow is added to the equation, however, consumers are able to spend far in excess of their after-tax incomes. For example, purchasing a home without the support of a mortgage would be out of reach for the typical individual or family. Think about how many years of saving hard-earned dollars it would take to meet the cost of a home in one lump-sum payment. In fact, most big-ticket items, like a car, involve borrowed money. Only a very few people can afford to pay cash.

It is important to view consumers' aggregate spending as composed of these two main components:

(1) Expenditures paid for out of after-tax income; and

(2) Expenditures financed by borrowed funds *(called credit-backed demand)*.

While a base level of spending within the economy is constantly being paid for with after-tax income, a portion is also being financed by bank lending or some type of similar credit source (credit cards, charge accounts, home equity loans, personal lines of credit, installment loans, automobile loans, and mortgages).

It is this second component of borrowing followed by spending that has grown as a portion of the total spending equation during the post-World War II era. Thus, we have become to a large degree a credit-functioning society that is greatly dependent on consumers' ability to borrow and repay credit–that is, we borrow until we can borrow no more (excess has become the American way). Then we stop borrowing and start repaying. We keep on paying down outstanding debt obligations until we are financially comfortable enough to borrow again.

Table 7.2 *Consumer Debt*

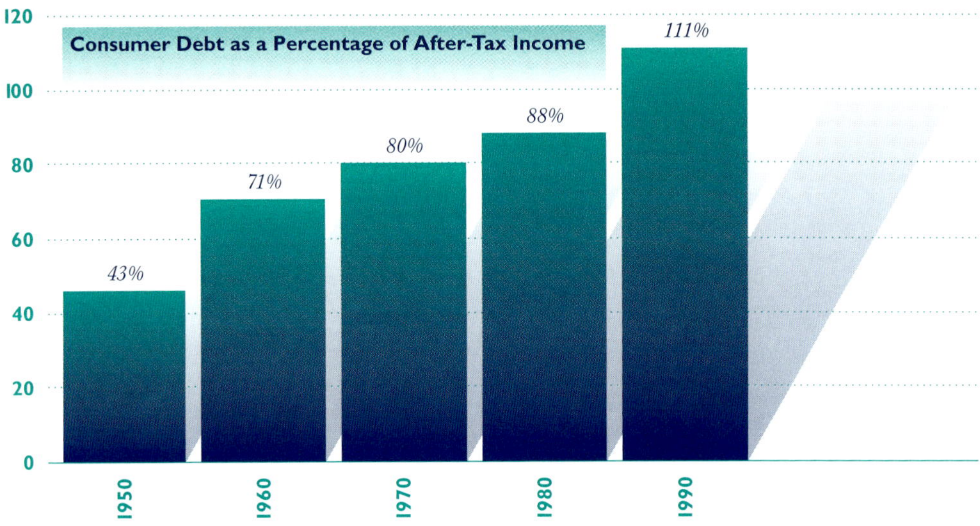

Source: Economic Report of the President, January, 1993.

Table 7.2 shows aggregate consumer debt by decade as a percentage of aggregate after-tax income for the country as a whole. Consumer debt includes nonmortgage debt (credit cards, personal lines of credit, installment loans, automobile loans, and charge accounts) and mortgage debt (mortgages for family homes, multifamily properties, and commercial properties).

The point is that credit-backed demand (consumer spending financed by borrowing) has been the key generator of inflation in the post-World War II era. Credit-backed demand has risen not primarily because there are more borrowers in the economy (leading to the overall higher level of total consumer debt), but because more borrowing is taking place per employed consumer.

As illustrated by Table 7.2, in 1950 total consumer debt as a percentage of aggregate after-tax income was only 43%, whereas by 1990 it represented 111%. This means that the country has more than doubled its debt load (the total amount of debt owed) over the forty-year period from 1950 to 1990. Moreover, as of 1990, it shows that, on average, Americans actually owe more in total debt than one year's after-tax income (the repayment source of that debt). This expansion in credit has had a negative impact on the American consumer's ability to save.

We should also mention that although credit was available prior to World War II, it was not available in the amounts and for the purposes that it is in the present day. Before World War II, most consumer debt consisted mainly of mortgage debt, with interest-only payments followed by a balloon payment (typically due in ten years or less). It was not until after World War II that credit became largely available for nonmortgage purposes, and this trend greatly accelerated in the 1970s.

The Business Cycle

It is important to understand that our economy functions within the constraints of the business cycle. As shown in Table 7.3, the business cycle has these four stages:

(1) Expansion,

(2) Peak,

(3) Contraction, and

(4) Trough.

In other words, our economy grows until it can grow no more. It then peaks, begins to contract and finally levels off at the bottom of the cycle (trough) until it subsequently begins expanding again. The performance of the economy throughout the business cycle is measured by monitoring the total output of all goods and services produced within the United States – the gross domestic product (GDP).

Table 7.3 *Economic Activity*

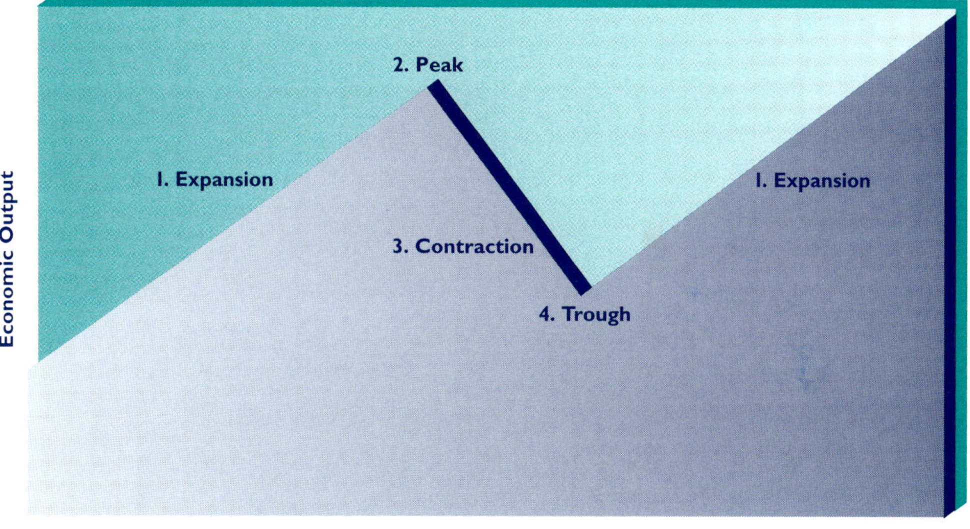

The business cycle since World War II has been largely affected by the consumer's ability to borrow and repay credit. This is because the economy, to a large extent, grows as long as consumer debt levels will support increased borrowing, which in turn finances increased spending and causes overall growth. As spending increases, the demand for goods and services begins to exceed supply, typically causing inflation to pick up. This is stage 1: Expansion.

Eventually, consumers become "borrowed up"–that is, they stop borrowing and start paying down their accumulated debt. As a result, borrowing slows, and so does the portion of total spending financed by borrowing. This is stage 2: Peak.

As after-tax income is directed toward repaying outstanding debts, demand slows, which causes an overall slowdown in the economy. This is stage 3: Contraction. Demand does continue, however, for items not financed by credit, such as food and other basic necessities, and some borrowing does occur but at a slower pace.

When inflation cools because of a slowdown in demand, unemployment picks up since the reduced demand for goods and services requires fewer workers. This results in a lower level of aggregate output (gross domestic product). The economy bounces along the bottom of the business cycle until consumer confidence returns. This is stage 4: Trough. At this stage, consumer confidence is usually very low.

If the slowdown in the economy is long enough that there are two back-to-back quarters of *negative growth in inflation-adjusted output* (called real output), the economy is said to be in a *recession*. Table 7.4 shows the length and depth of the recessions since World War II.

Table 7.4 *Recessions Since World War II*

	Recession Years	Duration in Months	Change in Real Output
1	1948–1949	11	-1.40%
2	1953–1954	10	-3.70
3	1957–1958	8	-3.90
4	1960–1961	10	-1.60
5	1969–1970	11	-1.00
6	1973–1975	16	-4.90
7	1980	6	-2.30
8	1981–1982	16	-3.30
9	1990–1991	8	-2.20

Source: Economic Report of the President, January, 1993.

As the table shows, there have been nine recessions since World War II, with the last one ending in 1991. Typically, slowdowns in the economy result in slowdowns in income and market performance. Therefore, as you examine family income and market performance later in this module, keep in mind when these recessions have occurred and how long they have lasted.

Monetary and Fiscal Policy

While the business cycle is continuous, it can be shaped and controlled to some extent by the actions of the Federal Reserve (the nation's central bank) and the joint actions of Congress and the President. The actions of the Federal Reserve Board (the governing body of the Federal Reserve) and its ability to influence interest rates is known as *monetary policy*. On the other hand, the joint actions of Congress and the President to tax and spend in an effort to steer economic activity set the country's *fiscal policy*.

In its simplest definition, monetary policy has to do with influencing the money supply and the direction of interest rates in order to encourage or discourage borrowing–all of which, in turn, increase or decrease the credit-backed portion of total spending. In its broadest application, monetary policy is used to stimulate spending during recessions. By increasing the money supply and lowering interest rates during recessionary periods, the Federal Reserve tries to encourage credit-backed spending to pull the economy upward. Conversely, monetary policy is also used to slow the economy down by raising interest rates and restricting money supply growth. When interest rates rise increasing the cost of borrowing, spending financed by credit usually slows down.

Fiscal policy has the same aim as monetary policy–that is, to influence economic activity–it just uses different mechanisms to do so. The two basic mechanisms behind fiscal policy are:

(1) Increasing or decreasing the amount of taxes paid (income, sales, license, property, or transfer tax); and

(2) Increasing or decreasing the amount of government spending.

Monetary policy (which works with interest rates) and fiscal policy (which works with taxes and spending) have the same goals. They are, however, merely tools the Federal Reserve Board, Congress, and the President use to help move the business cycle along. It takes time for these tools to produce results; even if monetary and fiscal policy changes are implemented, there is typically a lag before they take effect in the economy.

One final point about using monetary policy or fiscal policy to stimulate the economy: As consumers begin to spend, the demand for goods and services can start to exceed supply, thus generating inflation. This is a negative offshoot of the positive effects that monetary or fiscal policy can bring to a lagging economy. If inflation picks up too quickly as the business cycle begins to expand, monetary or fiscal policy changes will need to be adopted again. If so, it is likely that interest rates or taxes will be raised. Therefore, monetary and fiscal policy–either together or independently–act as a gas pedal or brake to the growth of the economy. The goal is to keep the economy growing at a speed that will not generate undue inflation–a difficult task.

Table 7.5 *Recap of Inflation Rates 1949–1994*

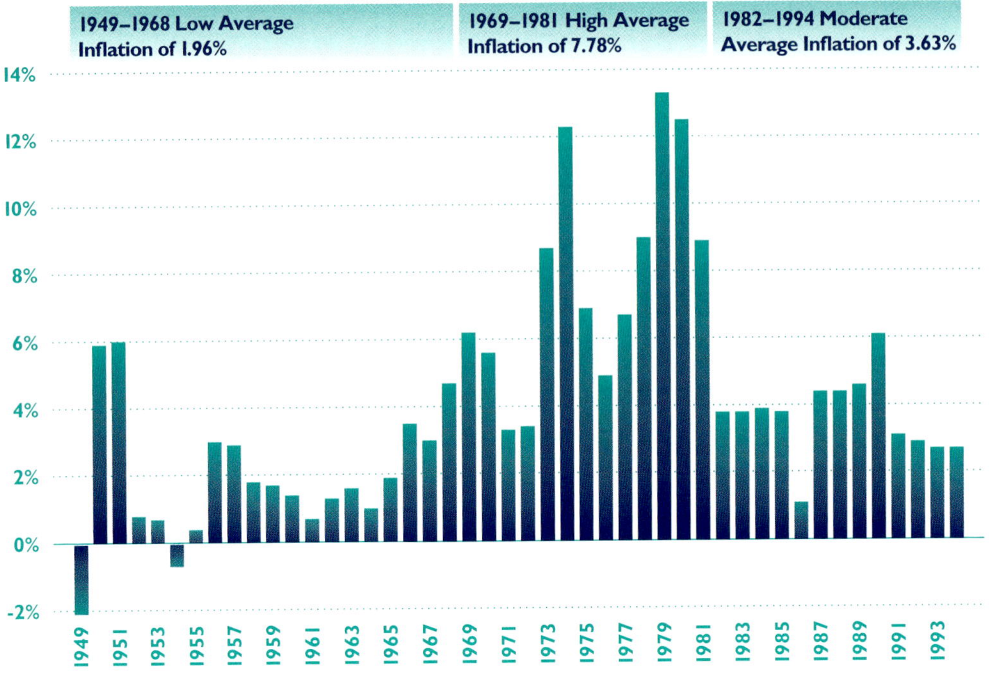

Source: U.S. Department of Labor, Bureau of Labor Statistics.

Table 7.5 presents the same three segments of time we described in Module 2:

(1) The twenty-year period of low inflation from 1949 through 1968;

(2) The thirteen-year period of high inflation from 1969 through 1981; and

(3) The thirteen-year period of moderate inflation from 1982 through 1994.

Now let's examine family income and the performance of the financial markets on an inflation-adjusted basis.

Family Income

As discussed in Module 2, two doublings have occurred in living costs (using 1949 as a base year). The first doubling took place at the end of 1974 and the second doubling at the end of 1982. As a result, family incomes–using median family income as our monitor–have had to increase significantly since World War II just to keep pace with inflation. The U.S. government defines median family income as follows:

- *Family* is a unit where two or more persons are related by birth, marriage, or adoption and are residing together.
- *Median* represents the middle point in the range of family incomes, that is, there are an equal number of family incomes above and below the midpoint figure. Note that the median is different from the average (which would be determined by totaling the numbers and then dividing the total by the number of incomes in the sample). Thus, the average family income is above the median, because very high incomes pull up the average. The median, therefore, is a less biased measure of family income performance.

Table 7.6 *Inflation-Adjusted Median Family Incomes 1950–1994*

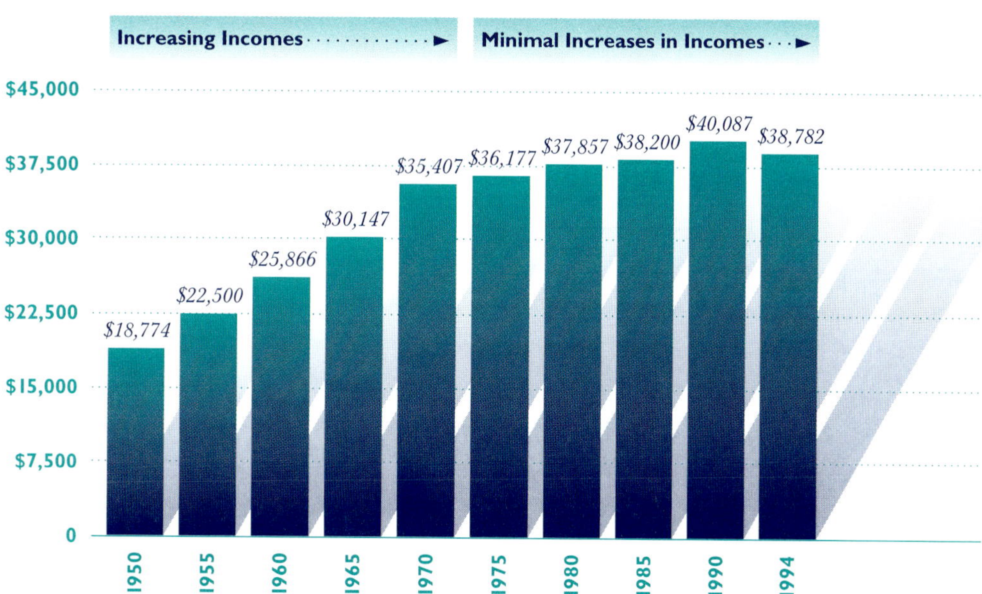

Source: U.S. Bureau of the Census, Current Population Reports, Series P-60.
Amounts expressed in terms of the purchasing power of a 1994 dollar.

Table 7.6 illustrates median family income for selected individual years from 1950 through 1994. The figures have all been adjusted for inflation according to the purchasing power of a 1994 dollar. This allows us to compare the numbers across time.

As we can see in the table, during 1950–1970 (a period of low inflation), median family incomes rose from $18,774 to $35,407, an 89% increase. Because this is the amount *after* adjusting for inflation, the increase is all the more significant. Now look at the next twenty-four-year period, 1970–1994, during which we experienced high inflation through 1981. Here, the results are quite different. By 1994, median family income had increased to only $38,782, after peaking at $40,087 in 1990, compared to the 1970 figure of $35,407. This represents an increase of only 10% over the twenty-four-year period. In summary, then, Table 7.6 shows that incomes were outpacing inflation during the 1950–1970 period, but were just keeping ahead of inflation during 1970–1994.

Table 7.7 *1994 Family Income Ranges*

Income range	Percent of families
Under $10,000	9%
$10,000 to $24,999	22%
$25,000 to $49,999	32%
$50,000 to $74,999	20%
Over $75,000	17%

Source: U.S. Bureau of the Census, Current Population Reports, Series P-60, Unpublished Data.

Now that we have illustrated median (midpoint) family income during the period from 1950 to 1994, let's examine the ranges of family income. Table 7.7 presents the actual (non-inflation-adjusted) family income ranges in 1994. As you can see, approximately 9% of all family incomes were under $10,000; 22% were in the $10,000 to $24,999 range; 32% were in the $25,000 to $49,999 range; 20% were in the $50,000 to $74,999 range; and 17% were over $75,000. Table 7.7 enables you to see where the income of a family unit (as previously defined in this section) fits within the income distribution ranges for 1994. This might help you understand how your family income is faring vis-avis other families throughout the country. Keep in mind that the data are for family incomes and that data for individuals will be different.

The Three Types of Investments

Our discussion now takes us to the financial markets. Despite the complexity of the financial markets, there are only three primary types of investments: (1) cash investments, (2) bond investments, and (3) stock investments. (Another investment, mutual funds, can be a participant individually in each of, or collectively in two or all three, investment types.) Let's discuss each of the three types of investments shown in Table 7.8.

Table 7.8 *The Three Types of Investments*

Cash Investments	Bond Investments	Stock Investments
1. Checking Accounts 2. Savings Accounts 3. Money Market Accounts 4. Certificates of Deposit	1. Government Bonds 2. Corporate Bonds 3. Tax-Exempt Bonds	1. Common Stocks 2. Preferred Stocks

Cash Investments

A cash investment is an investment that can be turned quickly into cash. All cash investments operate under the same basic principle of earning a relatively fixed annual rate of interest on the amount invested. Unfortunately, because they are very safe investments – the principal is not usually subject to loss – they provide low annual rates of return compared to other types of investments.

Cash investments include interest-bearing checking accounts, savings accounts, money market accounts (money market mutual funds), and certificates of deposit. Interest-bearing checking accounts, savings accounts, and money market accounts are basically the same as cash because the funds in these investments can be accessed immediately without penalty – thus the term cash investment. Certificates of deposit, on the other hand, although they are included in this category, are not really cash investments. Since certificates of deposit have a set maturity date and carry a penalty for early withdrawal, the money within these investments is not as readily accessible as other forms of cash investments (unless you are willing to pay the penalty for early withdrawal).

Bond Investments

Bond investments, the second major investment vehicle, include corporate bonds, govern- ment and government agency bonds, and tax-exempt bonds. Tax-exempt bonds are bond issued by municipalities as well as states, counties, and other taxing authorities. The incom from these bonds is free from federal, and possibly state and local, income taxes.

Unlike cash investments, bonds offer *two* forms of return. The first is the fixed interes payment on the bond (similar to the interest rate paid on a cash investment). The bond ca also increase or decrease in price after purchase, resulting in a gain or loss if the bond is sol prior to maturity. This gain or loss is the second form of return. If the bond is retained unti maturity, the owner is then paid par value (measured in $1,000 increments) regardless of th purchase price. This could also result in either a gain or loss depending on the purchas price you paid.

Changes in bond prices arise primarily from changes in interest rates. This is becaus the market price of bonds moves inversely to the direction of interest rate changes. If interes rates rise, bond prices fall; if interest rates fall, bond prices rise. Furthermore, the longer th life of the bond, the more its dollar value will react to interest rate changes–that is, the per centage increase or decrease will be greater. Table 7.9 offers a snapshot of the return fron interest income for each class of bonds in relation to one another.

Table 7.9 *Bond Yields*

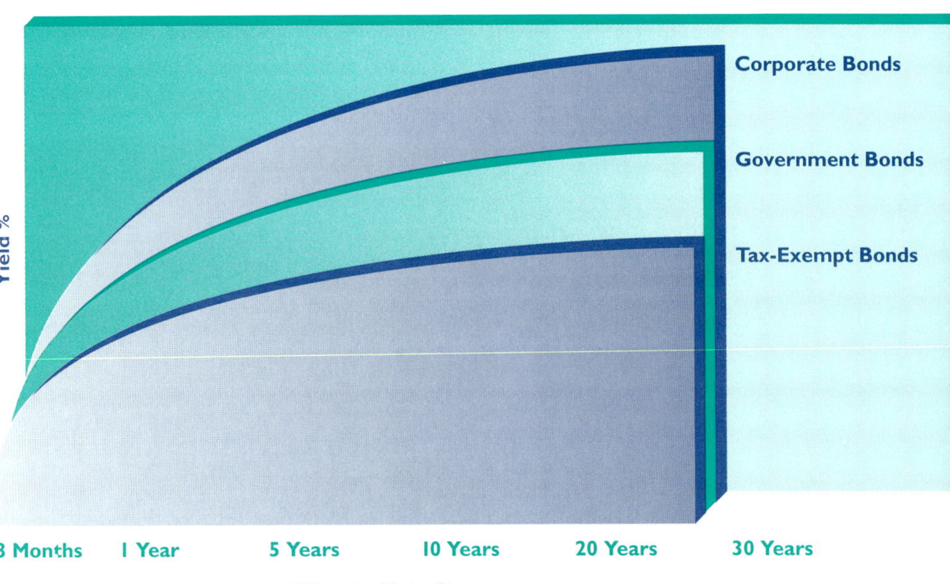

As the table shows, corporate bonds typically provide the highest yields (speaking here only of the interest-payment portion of total return), followed by government bonds, and finally tax-exempt bonds. Even though tax-exempt bond returns are lower, they can still be competitive with the after-tax returns of government and corporate bonds because they are free from federal, and possibly state and local, income taxes. Tax-exempt bonds are most frequently purchased by high-income taxpayers.

As the term to maturity increases, so does the bond's yield (percentage return). Along with the the longer term to maturity and the higher yield, however, also comes the possibility of the issuer defaulting on the interest payment or return of principal at maturity.

Let's take a look at how corporate and municipal bonds are rated. (Government bonds are not rated since there is no risk of default on the interest payments or the return of principal at maturity. This is because the federal government is the issuer, and it maintains the power to tax, borrow, or print money to meet its obligations.)

Table 7.10 *Bond Ratings*

		Standard & Poor's Rating	Rating Indicates	Moody's Rating
Investment Grade	1	AAA	Highest Quality	Aaa
	2	AA	High Quality	Aa
	3	A	Good Quality	A
	4	BBB	Medium Quality	Baa
	5	BB	Speculative Quality	Ba
	6	B	Speculative	B
	7	CCC	More Speculative	Caa
	8	CC	Highly Speculative	Ca
	9	D	In Default	–
	10	N	Not Rated	N

Table 7.10 summarizes the ratings of the top two bond rating services – Standard & Poor's (S&P) and Moody's Bond Service. Both companies are well-respected firms that track the bond market and the companies that issue bonds in these markets, and both rate bonds from highest-to-lowest credit quality. Both services' two lowest ratings represent bonds that are either in default – a bond that is not meeting its interest payments and potentially its payment of principal – or not rated – a bond about which there is not enough information to compile a rating.

Bonds that fall into the uppermost four categories for both services are referred to as investment grade. Investment-grade bonds are from medium to highest quality and therefore have a low chance of default risk. Bonds below investment grade are considered more speculative in nature and therefore have a greater chance of default risk. Because of the greater risks associated with such bonds, they pay higher interest (coupon) rates than investment-grade bonds. Knowing whether a bond is highly rated or poorly rated will give you a feel for the credit quality of a bond portfolio.

Stock Investments

Stocks, also called equities, are the third type of investment. There are only two types of stock investments: common stocks and preferred stocks. Like bonds, stocks also offer two potential forms of return. First, the stock can pay dividends (a return of corporate after-tax income), although this is not a required payment. Second, the stock can increase or decrease in price after it is purchased, resulting in a gain or loss in stock value. Note that the actual gain or loss in stock value is only truly incurred by the owner at the time the stock is sold.

While both common and preferred stocks provide ownership in the issuing corporation, preferred stocks differ from common stocks in two ways: (1) they provide a fixed payment, called a dividend, and (2) the price of the stock typically moves inversely to interest rate changes. Moreover, largely because of their favorable tax treatment, preferred stocks are held mostly by corporations as opposed to individuals.

The Three Markets

In the remainder of this module, we will discuss the cash investments market, the bond market, and the stock market. These three broad sectors make up the financial markets, with mutual funds participating in all three sectors. In the cash investment market we will examine the rates of a 30-day treasury bill (used here as a proxy for cash investments over time); in the bond market we will discuss long-term corporate bonds; and in the stock market we will review both large and small company stocks.

Over the long run, cash investments typically offer the lowest rates of return (in comparison to stocks and bonds); they also offer the least amount of risk. It is very rare to lose money placed in a cash investment. Bond investments offer higher rates of return than cash investments, and over the long run, stock investments can offer still greater returns than bond investments.

Along with higher potential returns, bond investments also carry a higher level of risk than cash investments because the market value of bonds can decline from their purchase price, or the bond issuer can default on interest or principal payment obligations. Stocks also carry the risk of declining market values. And, in addition, stocks have the potential for dividends to be reduced or eliminated. Therefore, as we examine the three markets, keep in mind that each market sector carries a different level of risk.

Cash and Bond Investments and the Business Cycle

As the business cycle moves through its four stages (expansion, peak, contraction, and trough), the demand for goods and services—fueled to a large degree by credit (borrowed money)—will rise and fall. As the demand for goods and services and with it the *demand for money* (borrowed funds) increases and decreases in tandem with the business cycle, so will the price of borrowed funds, which is measured by *the interest rate*. This is an important point.

Borrowed money is a commodity that has a price (the interest rate), just as tangible goods have a price. During economic expansion (when demand for goods and services exceeds supply), the cost of money rises. Economic expansion usually occurs because consumers begin borrowing at higher levels (increasing the credit-backed portion of total spending). Therefore, the demand for borrowed funds increases, causing the demand for credit to exceed the supply of credit. When the demand for credit is greater than the supply, the price of borrowed funds, as measured by the interest rate, begins to rise.

Typically, changes in interest rates occur when the Federal Reserve Board reacts to changes in inflation expectations through monetary policy. As the interest rate rises, so does the rate of return that is paid out on cash investments and bond investments. This is because the rate that must be paid to investors to attract their investment dollars rises as the cost of money rises. As a result, when the cost of money increases, not only does the cost of borrowing rise, but the rate of return offered to investors also rises. Similarly, when interest rates fall (representing a decrease in the cost of money), not only does the cost for borrowing fall, but the rate of return offered to investors also falls. In summary, therefore, interest rates and rates of return on cash and bond investments move together.

We will now examine the total returns for cash investments, long-term corporate bond investments, large company stocks, and small company stocks on *a pretax, inflation-adjusted basis* during the forty-six-year period from 1949 through 1994. We will use the pretax inflation-adjusted approach to expose the effects of inflation, which has been called the *hidden tax*. Although it does not reduce after-tax return, it *does* reduce purchasing power, which has a similar effect as decreasing after-tax return.

Table 7.11 *Inflation-Adjusted Total Returns for Cash Investments (1949–1994)*

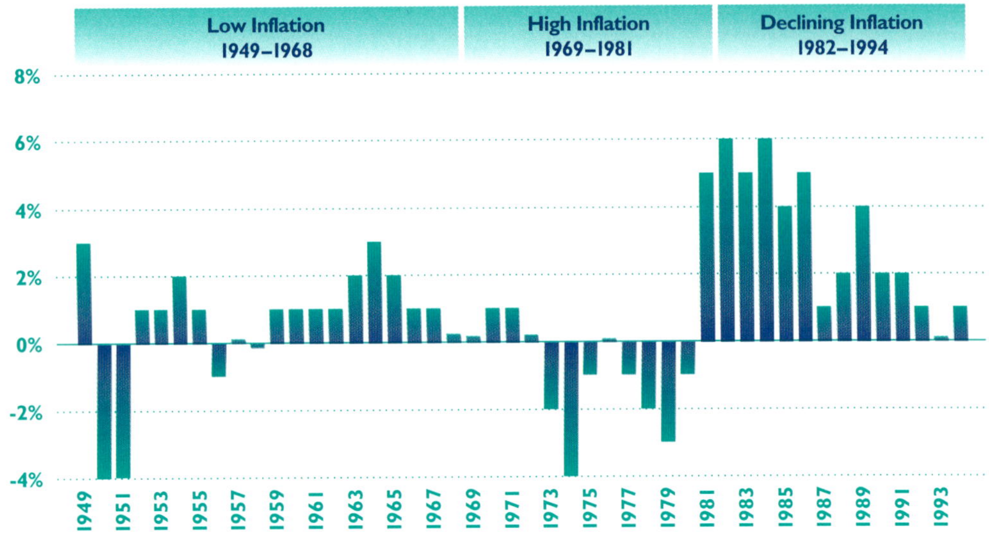

Source: © Stocks, Bonds, Bills, and Inflation 1995 Yearbook™, *Ibbotson Associates, Chicago (annually updates work by Roger G. Ibbotson and Rex A. Sinquefield). Used with permission. All rights reserved. Cash investments represented by 30-day Treasury bill rate, one bill portfolio.*

Table 7.11 shows the inflation-adjusted total returns for cash investments during the years 1949 through 1994. During 1949–1968, the inflation-adjusted returns were low (for the most part less than 2%). However, because the returns from cash investments in most years were *greater* than inflation, the inflation-adjusted returns, albeit low, were still positive. During 1969–1981, inflation picked up, causing several years of very low to negative inflation-adjusted returns because the returns offered from cash investments were near or below the rate of inflation. During 1982–1994, returns were above the annual rates of inflation, which produced positive inflation-adjusted returns. In addition, during the earlier portion of the 1982–1994 period, inflation began declining from its 1979–1981 highs at a faster pace than did returns on cash investments, increasing the inflation-adjusted returns.

Thus, 1949–1968 was a period of low inflation, 1969–1981 was a period of rising inflation, and 1982–1994 was period of declining inflation. Let's see the impact of these three periods on long-term corporate bonds.

Table 7.12 *Inflation-Adjusted Total Returns for Long-Term Corporate Bonds (1949–1994)*

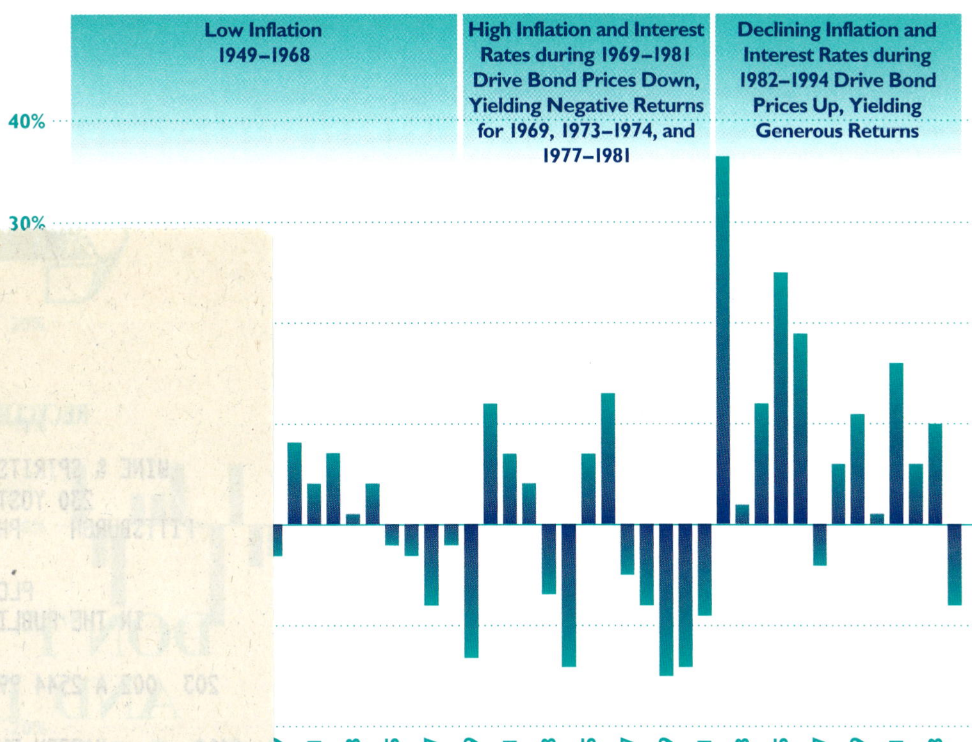

Inflation 1995 Yearbook™, *Ibbotson Associates, Chicago*
Ibbotson and Rex A. Sinquefield). Used with permission. All rights reserved.
by Salomon Brothers Long-Term High Grade Corporate Bond Index.

the inflation-adjusted total returns for long-term corporate bond orty-six-year period from 1949 through 1994. During 1949–1968, rns were low—usually under 10%, including some years with nega- increased during 1969–1981, there were some years with positive urns and some years with negative inflation-adjusted returns. Note the n that the positive returns followed by negative returns produced during 31 as a result of these interest rate swings.

For the most part, long-term bond returns were greater than inflation during 1982–1994. Inflation declined at a faster pace than returns on long-term corporate bond investments during the first several years of this period, bringing about positive inflation-adjusted returns. In 1982, the total return was 37%, and in many of the years that followed, there were double-digit returns. These high returns were due to declining interest rates, which marked the end of the rising inflation created during the latter part of the 1970s. Remember, when interest rates fall, bond prices rise, which boosts their *total* return.

Comparing bond investments to cash investments, we can see that bond returns are typically above cash investment returns because of the increased risk associated with bond investments. As we explained earlier, the total return for bonds consists of interest income plus (1) the difference between what you paid for the bond and par value (if the bond is held to maturity); or (2) the increase or decrease in the bond's market price compared with the purchase price (if the bond is sold). (Even though the returns from cash investments are also generated from underlying investments that change in price, the returns usually consist only of interest income.)

Table 7.13 *Inflation-Adjusted Total Returns for Large Company Stocks (1949–1994)*

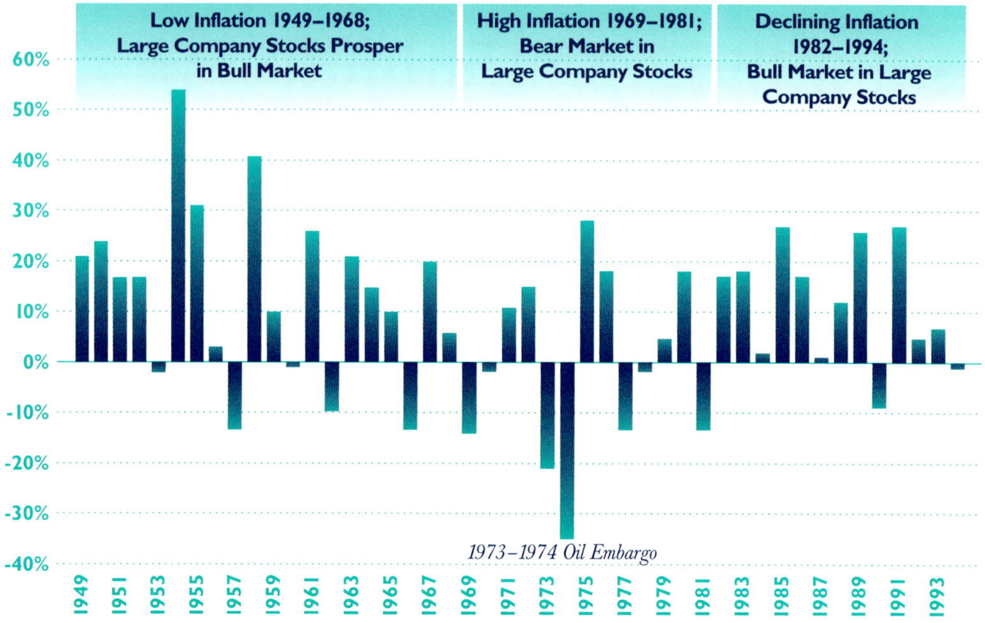

Low Inflation 1949–1968; Large Company Stocks Prosper in Bull Market

High Inflation 1969–1981; Bear Market in Large Company Stocks

Declining Inflation 1982–1994; Bull Market in Large Company Stocks

60%
50%
40%
30%
20%
10%
0%
-10%
-20%
-30%
-40%

1973–1974 Oil Embargo

1949 1951 1953 1955 1957 1959 1961 1963 1965 1967 1969 1971 1973 1975 1977 1979 1981 1983 1985 1987 1989 1991 1993

Source: © Stocks, Bonds, Bills, and Inflation 1995 Yearbook™, *Ibbotson Associates, Chicago (annually updates work by Roger G. Ibbotson and Rex A. Sinquefield). Used with permission. All rights reserved.*
Large company stocks represented by S&P 500 with dividends reinvested (S&P 500, 1957–1994; S&P 90, 1949–1956).

Now we'll look at large company stocks for the same forty-six-year period from 1949 through 1994, as illustrated in Table 7.13. Inflation-adjusted returns were mostly positive from 1949–1968, ranging from a high of 54% (1954) to a low of -13% (1957 and 1966). For large company stocks, most of this period was a bull market (where stock prices were generally rising).

From 1969 until 1981 inflation-adjusted returns were mixed positive and negative. During this period, large company stocks were in a long-term bear market (where stock prices were generally declining or providing little growth). The wavelike pattern produced by these positive returns followed by negative returns during 1969–1981 is much like the pattern during the same years for long-term bonds. During 1982–1994, inflation declined. This set the stage for another bull market in large company stocks where returns, for the most part, were positive and increasing.

Because of the increased risk associated with these investments, large company stock returns are typically higher than long-term corporate bond returns. (Remember that the total return for stocks consists of dividend income coupled with any increase or decrease in the price of the stock.)

Table 7.14 *Inflation-Adjusted Total Returns for Small Company Stocks (1949–1994)*

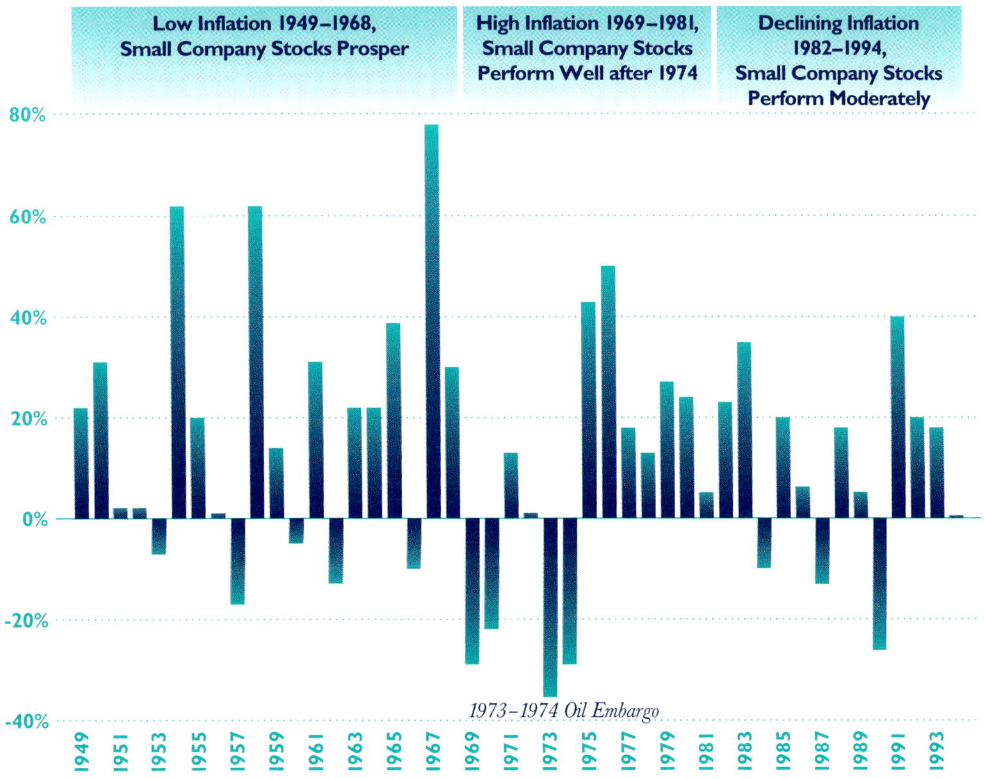

Low Inflation 1949–1968, Small Company Stocks Prosper

High Inflation 1969–1981, Small Company Stocks Perform Well after 1974

Declining Inflation 1982–1994, Small Company Stocks Perform Moderately

1973–1974 Oil Embargo

Source: © Stocks, Bonds, Bills, and Inflation 1995 Yearbook™, *Ibbotson Associates, Chicago (annually updates work by Roger G. Ibbotson and Rex A. Sinquefield). Used with permission. All rights reserved. Small company stocks represented by the fifth capitalization quintile of stocks on the NYSE for 1926–1981. Performance of the Dimensional Fund Advisors (DFA) Small Company Fund 1982–1994.*

Let's move on to the fourth category of investment: small company stocks. Table 7.14 shows the inflation-adjusted total returns for small company stocks from 1949 through 1994. In 1949–1968 – a bull market for stocks – total returns were primarily positive, ranging from a high of 78% (1967) to a low of -17% (1957).

As inflation picked up from 1969–1981, inflation-adjusted returns were mostly negative through 1974. However, beginning in 1975, returns for small company stocks reversed direction. This ushered in a continuing bull market in small company stocks, and returns were largely positive. Interestingly, during 1969–1981, small company stocks reported a total return of 254%, while large company stocks (which were experiencing a bear market during those years) reported a total return of 104%, less than half that of small company stocks. This occurred despite small company stocks' poor performance during 1969–1974.

Note that total returns for small company stocks are typically above large company stock returns; however, with the increased return comes increased variability and higher risk. Also note that small company stock returns don't always move in tandem with large company stocks. Sometimes while large company stocks are declining, small company stocks may be rising.

Table 7.15 *Non-Inflation-Adjusted and Inflation-Adjusted Average Returns (1949–1994)*

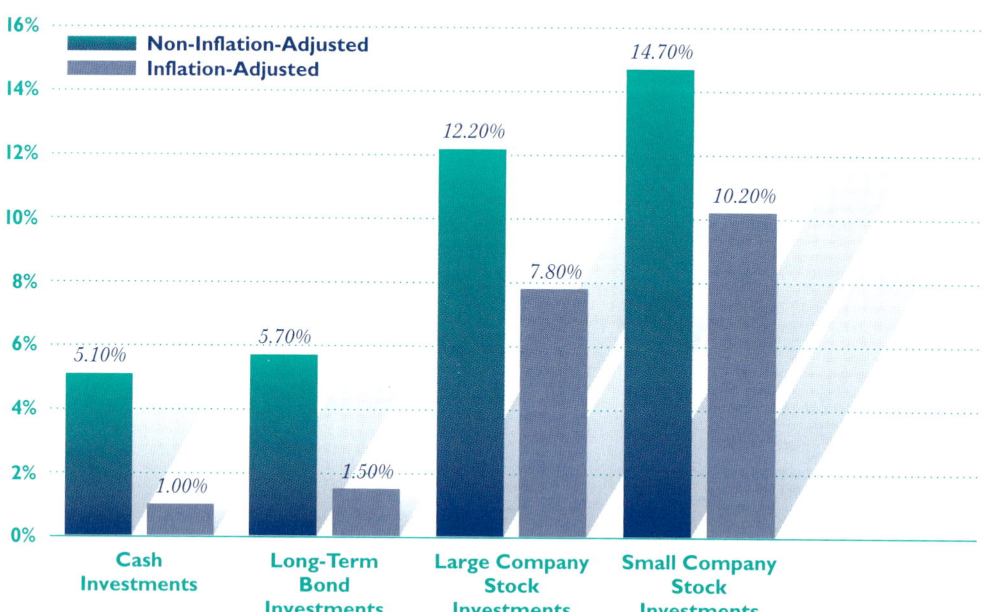

Source: © Stocks, Bonds, Bills, and Inflation 1995 Yearbook™, *Ibbotson Associates, Chicago (annually updates work by Roger G. Ibbotson and Rex A. Sinquefield). Used with permission. All rights reserved.*

Table 7.15 summarizes the average non-inflation-adjusted and inflation-adjusted returns for cash investments, long-term bond investments, large company stock investments, and small company stock investments during 1949–1994. In a nutshell, after factoring in inflation, the only markets in which to obtain substantial pretax returns are in large and small company stocks. The cash investments and long-term bond markets provide very low returns when adjusted for inflation. Moreover, the total returns would be even lower after payment of applicable income taxes.

The Dow Jones Industrial Average

The final topic in this module is the Dow Jones Industrial Average. If you're going to invest in the stock market, you will undoubtedly be interested in knowing how the market is performing over time. To do this, you will need to use a stock market index. Although there are a number of market indexes that monitor the stock market, we are going to discuss only the most popular and widely followed one–the Dow Jones Industrial Average.

Besides the Dow Jones Industrial Average (which tracks consumer goods and service companies), there is a Dow Jones Transportation Average (which tracks twenty air, rail, and trucking transportation companies), a Dow Jones Utility Average (which tracks fifteen energy companies providing gas and electric power), and a Dow Jones Composite Average (which provides the composite average for the companies in the Industrial, Transportation and Utility Averages).

The Dow Jones Industrial Average–which we will hereafter refer to as the Dow–includes thirty large company stocks–often referred to as "blue chip" companies or stocks–listed on the New York Stock Exchange. By tracking the 30 Dow stocks, we will be able to monitor approximately one-fourth of the market value of all companies listed on the New York Stock Exchange. The Dow is used as a benchmark (along with the S & P 500), for measuring the performance of large company stocks. It is a widely followed stock market indicator measuring the duration of past bull and bear markets and it is a yardstick against which many mutual funds track their performance.

The companies comprising the Dow Jones Industrial Average, which span a broad range of businesses, are listed in Table 7.16.

Table 7.16 *The 30 Dow Jones Industrials*

1	Allied Signal	16	Goodyear
2	Aluminum Company of America	17	IBM
3	American Express	18	International Paper
4	AT&T	19	McDonalds
5	Bethlehem Steel	20	Merck
6	Boeing	21	J. P. Morgan
7	Caterpillar	22	Minnesota Mining and Manufacturing
8	Chevron	23	Phillip Morris
9	Coca Cola	24	Procter & Gamble
10	Disney	25	Sears, Roebuck & Company
11	DuPont	26	Texaco
12	Eastman Kodak	27	Union Carbide
13	Exxon	28	United Technologies
14	General Electric	29	Westinghouse Electric
15	General Motors	30	Woolworth

The Price Earnings Ratio (P/E) and Dividend Yield (DY)

Our study of the Dow will require using two key indicators that are referred to on business news broadcasts and in business papers and periodicals to analyze the Dow's performance: (1) the price earnings ratio (P/E); and (2) the dividend yield (DY).

The price/earnings ratio shows the relationship between a company's market price and its after-tax profits on a per-share basis. Let's look at an example. If the current market price of a stock is $10 per share and the earnings per share is $1, then the price/earnings ratio is 10 (10 divided by 1). The higher the P/E ratio, the more the investor is paying for a share of stock as a multiple of earnings per share. If earnings are $1 per share, a P/E of 20 means that an investor would be paying $20 for a share of stock (20 times earnings).

It may be helpful to think of the P/E ratio as the relative *price tag* on a company's stock. The P/E ratio, therefore, helps an investor determine whether a stock is undervalued (a good time to buy), overvalued (the stock is too expensive; time to sell), or fairly valued (buying opportunities require careful analysis, but they are fair). The P/E ratio allows an investor to determine how expensive a stock is not only in relation to its own past performance, but also in relation to other companies in its industry (by comparing their P/E ratios) and to the overall stock market (by using the P/E of the Dow).

The second key indicator is the dividend yield. A stock's potential overall return is a combination of price appreciation (the increase in stock price) and dividend income. Dividends are the portion of annual after-tax corporate profits returned to the shareholder on a per-share basis. For example, if a quarterly dividend were declared of 25 cents per share, a shareholder owning 1 share would receive a total annual dividend of $1. The dividend yield expresses the dividend per share in percentage terms by translating dividend return (on a per-share basis) into a percentage yield. The DY is determined by dividing a stock's annual dividend by its market price. If the annual dividend of $1 is paid while the stock's market price is $20, then the dividend yield is 5% ($1 divided by $20). Therefore, the dividend yield measures the return on a stock investment arising *from the dividend portion only.*

The DY makes it very easy to determine if the dividend being paid on a stock is attractive. For example, if certificates of deposit (as an alternative investment) were yielding 3% and the dividend on the stock mentioned above was 5%, obviously the stock would be paying a higher yield. However, this higher yield of 5% is accompanied by additional risk–that is, the stock could decline in value, but the certificate of deposit would remain a stable investment.

Still, the stock's 5% DY, coupled with its potential to increase in value above $20 make it appealing. Keep in mind, though, that as the stock's price rises, the dividend as a percentage of the stock's price (the dividend yield) will decline (unless the dividend rises).

The Dow 1949–1994

Now let's look at a graphic illustration of the Dow during 1949–1994. Recall that we are using the Dow to represent the overall stock market for large company stocks. As we review the performance of the Dow, we will also discuss its price earnings ratios and dividend yields.

As you will find out, price earnings ratios of approximately seven to eight times earnings (representing an *undervalued* stock market) have usually signaled the beginning of long-term primary bull markets. Price earnings ratios of approximately 20 to 21 times earnings (representing an *overvalued* stock market) have heralded the end of long-term primary bull markets.

Typically, dividend yields of approximately 7% (representing an *undervalued* stock market) have also signaled the beginnings of long-term primary bull markets in the past. Conversely, dividend yields approximating 3% (representing an *overvalued* stock market) have marked the end of long-term primary bull markets.

Table 7.17 *Dow Jones Industrial Average (1949–1994)*

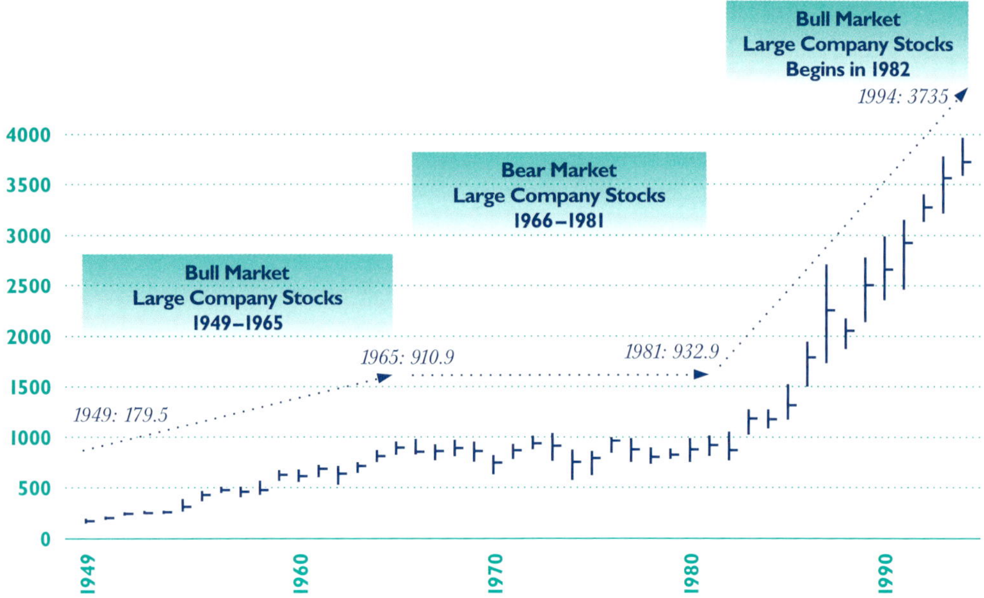

Source for numerical values: Copyright 1995 by Value Line Publishing, Inc. Reprinted by Permission; All Rights Reserved.

Above each year in Table 7.17 is a vertical line that indicates the span between that year's high and low Dow reading. The horizontal line (which looks like a small flag) on the right side of each vertical line points to the average reading of the Dow for that year. By referring to Table 7.17, it is immediately apparent that the seventeen-year bull market during 1949 through 1965 was an upward-trend market, the sixteen-year bear market during 1966–1981 was a relatively flat market, and the bull market that emerged in 1982 and has continued through 1994 was again an upward-trend market. The average price of the Dow was 179.5 in 1949, 910.9 in 1965, 932.9 in 1981, and 3735 in 1994.

Table 7.18 *Adding P/E Ratios and Dividend Yields to Dow (1949–1994)*

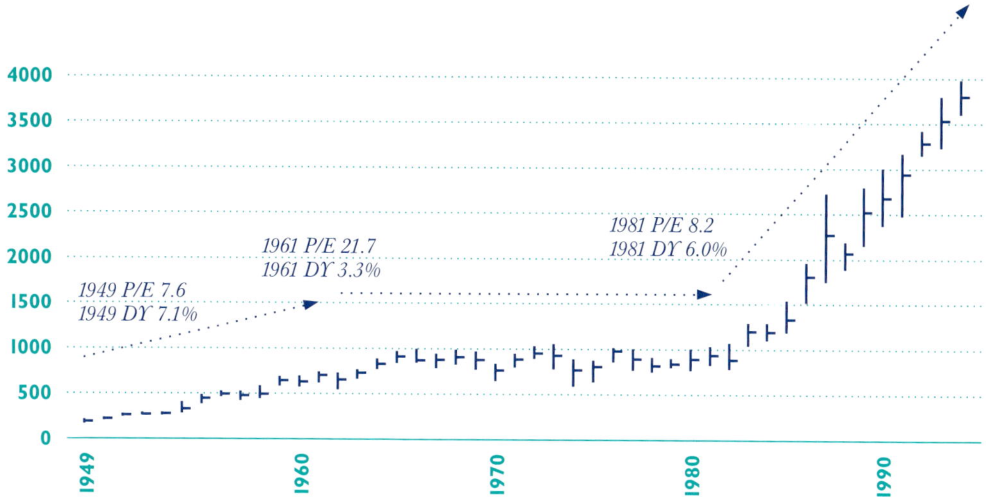

Source for numerical values: Copyright 1995 by Value Line Publishing, Inc. Reprinted by Permission; All Rights Reserved.
P/E represents price earnings ratio. DY represents dividend yield.

Table 7.18 adds P/E ratios and dividend yields to the Dow averages for the large company stock market graphed in Table 7.17. In 1949, the price earnings ratio of the Dow was 7.6 times the 1949 earnings–a relatively low multiple–while the dividend yield was 7.1%, an attractive yield. These two indicators, therefore, reflected that the market was under priced.

By 1965, the price earnings ratio of the Dow was 21.7 times the 1965 earnings–a high multiple–while the dividend yield had dropped to 3.3%–not as attractive a yield as in 1949. Thus, these two indicators denoted to market technicians that the market was becoming expensive as a multiple of earnings and that with the increase in market price, the dividend payout was low.

The Dow's P/E ratio had declined to 8.2 times earnings by 1981–a low multiple–while the dividend yield had increased to 6%–almost as attractive as the 1949 yield. These two indicators were again demonstrating that the market was underpriced–that is, the P/E was low and the DY was high.

When you listen to business news or read market commentaries, you will often be confronted with discussions on what the market has done historically and where it will be going in the future. These discussions will continually refer to the Dow's price, price earnings ratio, and dividend yield to evaluate the large company stock market. This review of the Dow should help you understand those discussions of market performance.

In the last portion of this module, let's see how recessions have affected the performance of the large company stock market during 1949-1994 as measured by the Dow and shown in Table 7.19.

Table 7.19 *Recessionary Effects on the Dow 1949–1994*

	Recession	Market Type	Dow Prior to Recession	Dow at End of Recession	Dow Increase (Decrease)	Percent Increase (Decrease)
1	1948–1949	Bull	177.6	179.5	1.9	1.07%
2	1953–1954	Bull	270.8	333.9	63.1	23.30
3	1957–1958	Bull	493.0	491.7	-1.3	-0.26
4	1960–1961	Bull	632.1	691.5	59.4	9.40
5	1969–1970	Bear	906.0	753.2	-152.8	-16.87
6	1973–1975	Bear	949.1	802.5	-146.6	-15.45
7	1980	Bear	844.4	891.4	47.0	5.57
8	1981–1982	Bear/Bull	891.4	884.4	-7.0	-0.79
9	1990–1991	Bull	2510.0	2933.0	423.0	16.85

Source for average Dow readings: Copyright 1995 by Value Line Publishing, Inc. Reprinted by Permission; All Rights Reserved.
All Dow citations are figures for the year prior to the year in which the recession began and for the year in which the recession ended.

The table covers both bull and bear markets, but as you will quickly see, bull markets are much less susceptible to recessions than bear markets.

Look at the far right column in the table (the percent change in the average reading of the Dow). The Dow actually *increased* at the end of each recession during the bull market of 1949 to 1965. Only during the 1957–1958 and the 1981–1982 recessions were there *decreases* during a bull market, and even so, each decrease was under 1% (1982 marked the end a long-term bear market and the emergence of a bull market).

However, during the bear market of 1966–1981, the Dow experienced much more severe declines–especially during the 1969–1970 and 1973–1975 recessions. It had a slight increase after the 1980 mini recession but then experienced a decrease from the effects of the 1981–1982 recession. By the end of the 1990–1991 recession, the Dow had increased 16.85%. From an historical standpoint, therefore, declines in a primary bear market, such as those that occurred during the 1966 to 1981 bear market, were much more severe than the declines that occurred in the primary bull market of 1949–1965.

One final note regarding the 1973–1974 decline: The percentage loss in the Dow from the opening of 1973 to the close of 1974 was 39.59%. *This is the greatest percentage loss in one period since World War II.* The severity of the 1973–1974 stock market decline can be attributed to two main factors: the Arab oil embargo of 1973–1974 and the subsequent collapse of investor confidence. During this severe decline, secondary stocks (stocks outside of the Dow) declined substantially more than those of the Dow.

Family Incomes and Stock Market Performance

As we conclude this module, it is important to note that much of the twenty-year period from 1949 to 1968 consisted of increasing inflation-adjusted median family incomes and a healthy large company stock market. This allowed families to improve their standard of living and invest in a market that was performing strongly. Beginning with the 1970s and continuing through 1994, however, family incomes increased only minimally on an inflation-adjusted basis. The large company stock market (as measured by the Dow), on the other hand, experienced a bear market from 1966–1981 and then entered a bull market in 1982 that has continued through 1994. It is important that you understand these economic cycles and the returns offered by past markets in order for you to be able to construct an intelligent financial plan.

Module 8 introduces you to mutual funds. They are the primary investment vehicle used with this financial planning system. Why invest with mutual funds you might ask? That question will be explored in greater detail in this module. The answer lies largely with the fact that many investors prefer delegating the responsibility of investing to professional fund managers.

Professional mutual fund managers devote themselves daily to managing portfolios, a task which can be difficult for individuals who lack the time or expertise. Even more importantly, professional fund managers can achieve broader diversification than most individuals assembling a portfolio of securities. The greater diversification that mutual funds can provide helps reduce the risks of investing in the financial markets.

What Is a Mutual Fund?

A mutual fund, also called an open-end investment company, is a corporation or business trust that invests and then manages money on an ongoing basis for individuals and businesses. The fund is owned at inception by its originating shareholders, who elect a board of directors. The board decides who will be in charge of running the fund–either officers of the company or a management company. Table 8.1 shows how the number of mutual funds has grown from 98 in 1950 to 5,357 at the end of 1994.

Table 8.1 *Number of Mutual Funds 1950–1994*

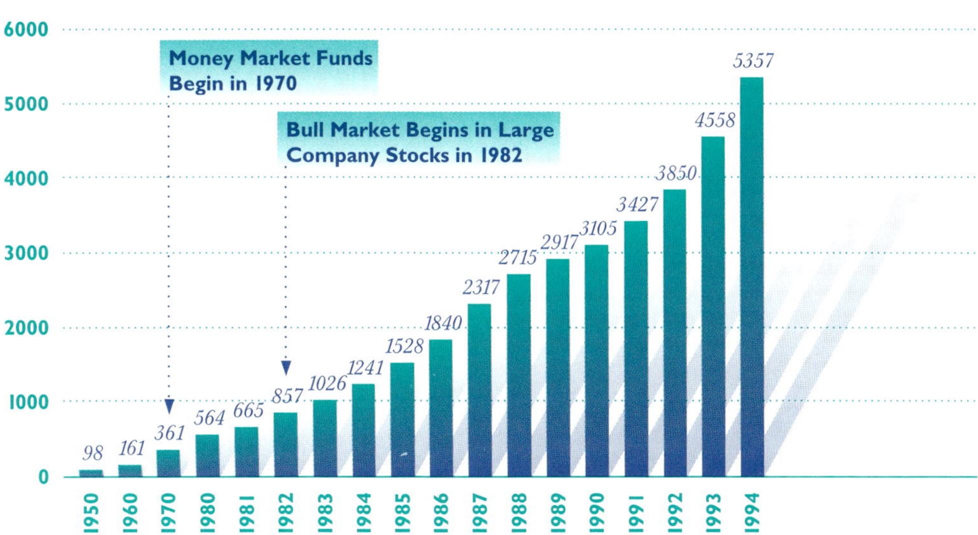

Source: Investment Company Institute

Mutual Fund Shares

As part of the process of starting a mutual fund, shares of the mutual fund company are sold to the public. By selling shares, the fund receives cash and the purchaser acquires ownership in the company. The mutual fund then buys any combination or individual selection of domestic or international stocks, bonds, or money market instruments.

As a result of the fund's ownership of these securities, earnings distributions to the shareholder can arise from:

(1) Interest paid on money market instruments or bonds,

(2) Dividends paid on stocks, and

(3) Net gains from the sale of securities.

These earnings distributions, which are paid out on a per-share basis, can be paid to the shareholder or reinvested to buy more shares. Thus the shareholder owning just a few shares receives the same *percentage* distribution as someone owning many shares.

Net Asset Value

When calculating the per-share value of a mutual fund, the first thing to keep in mind is that each share represents ownership in a portfolio of securities that can consist of any combination or individual selection of stocks, bonds, or money market instruments. The values of each security are added together to determine the total value of the portfolio.

Taking this value and reducing it by any liabilities the fund may owe equals the *net asset value* of the total portfolio. Dividing the total portfolio's net asset value by the total number of shares outstanding (shares held by investors) results in the *net asset value per share*. For example, if a mutual fund has total security holdings of $1,010,000 and liabilities of $10,000, the net asset value of the portfolio is $1,000,000. Dividing $1,000,000 by the number of shares outstanding—100,000 in this example—equals $10 per share. The net asset value then increases or decreases as the market value of the portfolio, total liabilities, or the number of shares outstanding changes. Table 8.2 illustrates this concept.

Table 8.2 *Net Asset Value Calculation*

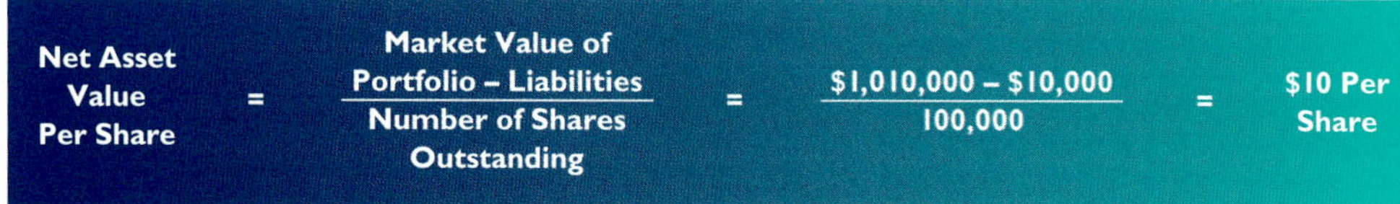

Buying and Selling Mutual Fund Shares

Mutual funds make direct and continual offerings of their shares to the investment public and at the same time stand ready to repurchase shares directly. This is accomplished by keeping an inventory of shares on hand to meet buyers' demands and enough cash to purchase sellers' shares.

As the fund purchases back shares of a mutual fund, cash must be available to pay the exiting shareholder. This, at times, requires the sale of securities within the portfolio to generate cash. At the same time, as shares are purchased from a mutual fund, the investment manager is responsible for investing the incoming cash. This buying and selling process is generally continued regardless of the condition of the financial markets (whether or not it is a good time to buy or sell securities).

Table 8.3 *Different Categories of Mutual Funds*

	1	2	3	4	5	6
Type of Fund	**Money Market Funds**	**Tax-Exempt Funds**	**Fixed-Income Funds**	**Growth and Income Funds***	**Growth Funds**	**Aggressive Growth Funds**
Objective	Stability and Income	Tax-free Income	Income	Growth and Income	Growth	Aggressive Growth
Primary Type of Investor	All Types	High-Tax Bracket Retirees	Retirees	Short-Term Investor (0–5 Years)	Medium-Term Investor (5–10 Years)	Long-Term Investor (over 10 Years)
Risk and Return	Low	Low to Medium	Low to Medium	Medium	High	Very High
Annual Range of Returns	1% to 15%	-18% to 48%	-8% to 43%	-15% to 32%	-26% to 53%	-31% to 84%
Annualized Return	5.10%	3.60%	5.70%	9.20%	12.20%	14.70%
Risk	Low ······► Medium ······► High					

Source: © Stocks, Bonds, Bills, and Inflation 1995 Yearbook™, *Ibbotson Associates, Chicago (annually updates work by Roger G. Ibbotson and Rex A. Sinquefield). Used with permission. All rights reserved. Data are for the period 1949–1994.*
**Portfolio rebalanced annually.*

Table 8.3 lists various categories of mutual funds, their objectives, the type of investor who typically purchases each category of fund, the category's risk and return relationship, and the annual pretax range of returns and annualized (average) return for each category for the period from 1949 to 1994. You'll notice that these ranges run from negative to positive for most fund types. An explanation of what we mean by risk and how to interpret the risk and return categorizations which appear in Table 8.3 is in order here. Each fund category has an inherent risk associated with it based on the types of securities purchased for its portfolio and the potential for those securities to either decline in price or in the dividend paid, or to default on interest or principal payments.

In addition, each category of fund has a relative risk associated with it vis-a-vis other fund types. For example, money market funds, because they are primarily invested in short-term, liquid securities have both an inherently low risk as well as a relatively low risk when compared with other mutual fund types.

Let's take a closer look.

Category 1: Money Market Funds

Category 1 is money market funds. The objective of these funds is typically to keep the principal (invested amount) stable and to generate income. Income from these funds is usually taxed at the federal level and at the state and local levels as applicable. As we just noted, the risk level and returns, compared to alternate fund investments, are low.

Category 2: Tax-Exempt Funds

Category 2 is tax-exempt funds. The objective of these funds is to produce tax-free income. Appreciation in the value of the underlying securities in the fund provides a secondary source of income. Tax-exempt funds, depending on the types of securities held, can be exempt from federal income taxes, from federal and state income taxes, or in some cases from federal, state, and local income taxes. Note that while income from tax-exempt funds may be non-taxable, capital gains arising from tax-exempt securities or funds is subject to applicable income taxes. Investors owning tax-exempt funds may have income distributions and, to a smaller extent, capital gains that are reportable and taxable.

The investments typically used to generate a tax-exempt fund's income are bonds offered by municipalities and townships. This type of fund, because of its tax-free status, generally offers a lower return than its taxable counterparts. Therefore, it is best suited for high-bracket taxpayers. This is because the fund's returns, depending on the investor's tax bracket, can be greater than the after-tax returns of taxable income funds. These funds are classified as low to medium risk.

Category 3: Fixed-Income Funds

The objective of the funds in category 3 – fixed-income funds – is generally to produce income. As with tax-exempt funds, appreciation of the underlying securities in the fund is a secondary source of income. The income from fixed-income funds is typically taxed at the federal level and at the state and local levels as applicable.

Usually, the investments used to generate the fixed-income fund's income are a blend of government and corporate bonds. By owning fixed-income funds, the investor has the potential for income distributions and, to a lesser degree, capital gains. These types of funds, which usually have a higher return (which is taxable) than their tax-free counterparts, are also classified as low to medium risk.

Category 4: Growth and Income Funds

Growth and income funds, category 4, are often referred to as balanced funds. The objective of these funds is to produce both capital growth and income. The growth side of the portfolio typically arises from ownership of stocks, while the income side is usually generated from bonds. The earnings from these funds are taxed at the federal level and also, when applicable, at the state and local levels.

Normally, the investments used to generate a growth and income fund's income are a combination of government and corporate bonds and common and preferred stocks of medium- to large-size companies. As with tax-exempt and fixed-income funds, owning growth and income funds creates the potential for the investor to have income distributions and capital gains. Usually classified as medium risk, growth and income funds are especially recommended for people who want some exposure to stocks but who will be investing for periods of five years or less.

Category 5: Growth Funds

Category 5 is growth funds. Since the objective of these funds is growth, it generally means that income will be minimal. The earnings and capital gains from these funds are usually taxed at the federal level and at the state and local levels as applicable.

Common and preferred stocks, typically of small to large companies, are the investments generally used to generate a growth fund's income. Owners of growth funds are pursuing the possibility of capital gains; income is a secondary concern. Usually classified as high risk, growth funds are recommended for individuals investing for at least five to ten years who want exposure to stocks.

Category 6: Aggressive Growth Funds

Aggressive growth is the objective for the funds in category 6, which generally means that there will be minimal to no income. These funds' earnings are taxed at the federal level and at the state and local levels as applicable.

Normally, the stocks of small- to medium-size emerging companies are the investments used to generate the aggressive growth fund's return. These companies do not generally pay dividends but reinvest their earnings back into the company to propel growth.

Owning aggressive growth funds creates the potential for large capital gains over time. These types of funds are typically classified as very high risk. This high risk stems from the fact that many companies in the portfolio are fledgling companies.

Aggressive growth funds are recommended for people who want exposure to stocks and will be investing for periods exceeding ten years. As noted in Table 8.3, the average return for this type of fund was 14.7% during 1949–1994. However, there have been years when annual returns dipped to minus 31% and other years when returns climbed to as high as 84%–it's a real roller coaster ride.

Other Types of Funds

While Table 8.3 shows the six broad categories of mutual funds, there are also a number of other types of funds. Sector funds, which specialize in certain markets, such as the health care industry or precious metals, are one example. Also, in recent years, highly specialized "affinity" funds have emerged targeted at investors who want their portfolio of investments to reflect their political or environmental concerns. There are also index funds, which attempt to hold the individual securities in major indexes such as the Dow Jones Industrial Average or the S&P 500.

A newer type of fund in the mutual fund marketplace–asset-allocation funds, also known as all-weather funds–is another example. This type of fund is a blend of stock, bond, and money market funds. Its purpose is to create a risk-reward relationship that is appropriate for the investor. Conservative asset-allocation funds invest a larger percentage of the portfolio in money market and bond investments; more aggressive asset allocation funds invest a larger percentage of the portfolio in stocks. (See Module 9 for a thorough explanation of asset allocation.)

We should also mention international funds. International mutual funds invest in securities abroad, and there is basically a comparable international fund for each type of domestic fund.

Total Pretax Return

Now let's move on to calculating total return. Mutual funds provide a total return that is made up of *dividend distributions* and *increases in share value*. Distributions are usually taxable to the shareholder in the year he or she receives them, while increases in share value (net asset value) are taxed when shares are sold.

Dividend distributions, also referred to as earnings distributions, can consist of:

(1) Investment income from interest paid on money market instruments, interest paid on bonds, and dividends paid on stocks; and

(2) Net capital gain income (the difference between securities sold for a profit and those sold for a loss).

Increases in share value result from unrealized gains on securities held by the fund or realized gains not yet distributed to shareholders. The term "unrealized" indicates that a security has not yet been sold. The term "realized" denotes that the security has been sold, whether for a profit or a loss.

Dividend distributions from a mutual fund can either be reinvested in the fund to buy more shares or passed directly to the shareholder. Table 8.4 shows the formula for determining the total pretax return when the dividend distributions are returned to the investor rather than reinvested into the fund each year.

Table 8.4 *Pretax Return for One Year (Distributions Not Reinvested)*

$$\text{Total Rate of Return for a Mutual Fund} = \left[\frac{(\text{Ending NAV} - \text{Beginning NAV}) + \text{Distributions}}{\text{Beginning NAV}}\right] \times 100$$

Let's use this formula in an example. If a mutual fund has a beginning net asset value (NAV) of $10.00, an ending net asset value of $10.50, and dividend distributions of $.40, then the total rate of return for the year will be as follows:

$$\text{Total Rate of Return for a Mutual Fund} = \left[\frac{(\$10.50 - \$10.00) + .40}{\$10.00}\right] \times 100 = 9.00\%$$

In this example, the dividend distributions are not reinvested. If they are reinvested, however, they will purchase more shares. These shares will then participate in the subsequent performance of the fund. Let's see how that works.

During the course of each year, mutual funds make distributions. The shareholder has the option to receive these distributions in cash or to have the distributions reinvested to buy more shares. If the distributions are used to buy more shares, the fund will automatically buy as many shares as it can with the dividend distributions.

For example, if a mutual fund owner holds 20 shares with a net asset value of $10 per share, the total value of shares is $200. If the fund makes a dividend distribution of $.50 per share, then our investor will have a $10.00 pretax return that can be paid to the shareholder or reinvested.

If the $10.00 is reinvested, it will buy as many shares as possible, based on the net asset value per share *after the distribution date*. (Note: Some funds reinvest at the net asset value on the date of distribution–prior to reducing the NAV by the distribution amount. Consequently, the NAV share price is higher and the reinvested dividends will purchase fewer shares.)

Continuing with our example, because the fund has a $10 net asset value prior to the date of distribution and then declares a $.50 dividend per share, the fund's net asset value after the distribution is $9.50. The $10.00 dividend distribution (20 shares multiplied by $.50 per share) will therefore purchase slightly more than one share (1.05 shares to be exact, $10 divided by $9.50), based on the the fund's net asset value after the date of distribution. Assume that the fund's NAV increases to $10.50 by the end of the year. Let's calculate the total return using the formula in Table 8.5.

Table 8.5 *Total Return Calculation with Dividends Reinvested*

$$\text{Total Rate of Return for a Mutual Fund with Dividends Reinvested} = \left[\frac{(\text{Year-End Shares} \times \text{Ending Year NAV}) - (\text{Start-of-Year Shares} \times \text{Beginning Year NAV})}{(\text{Start-of-Year Shares} \times \text{Beginning Year NAV})}\right] \times 100$$

The total return for our example fund is as follows:

$$\text{Total Rate of Return for a Mutual Fund with Dividends Reinvested} = \left[\frac{(21.05 \times \$10.50) - (20 \times \$10.00)}{(20 \times \$10.00)}\right] \times 100 = 10.51\%$$

Thus, our mutual fund earned a 10.51% return for the year. This return was achieved by reinvesting the $.50 per share dividend distribution ($10.00 total) into the fund when the net asset value was $9.50 ($10.00 predistribution NAV minus the .$50 per share distribution amount) along with the subsequent appreciation in the fund's NAV of $1.00 per share to $10.50 per share.

The Costs of Mutual Fund Investing

In many cases, mutual fund ownership involves costs over and above the net asset value. These costs are referred to as loads (sales loads) and can either be an upfront fee built into the share's purchase price or an add-on fee when shares are sold. These costs are usually used to pay a commission to the broker (salesperson) who sells the mutual fund to the investor and to pay a fee to the fund company. Loads typically range anywhere from 0 to 8.5% and are determined as a percentage of the offering price.

The cost of mutual fund investing can be broken down into three components:

(1) The base cost of a share of a mutual fund, which is its NAV;

(2) Sales charges of the fund (sales loads) that are added to the cost of shares either at the time of purchase or at the time of sale; and

(3) The expenses that are incurred in operating the fund, which are a charge against the fund's earnings. Assuming that the sales charge is applied at the time of purchase, we'll now illustrate how these costs affect share value.

If you purchased one share of a mutual fund that had (1) an offering (purchase) price of $10.50 per share, (2) a 5% upfront load included in the purchase price, and (3) a 1% charge for expenses associated with running the fund in a particular year (called management and administrative fees), the following would occur: First, you would pay $10.50 for one share. Second, the sales load would be $.525 ($10.50 x 5%), and the net asset value of your investment would be $9.975 ($10.50 – $.525) Third, you would be charged approximately $.10 ($9.975 x 1%) by the fund for the management of your money.

Therefore, your $10.50 investment would be worth only $9.875 ($10.50 – $.525 – $.10). The fund would have to earn a total return of $.625 to increase the net value of your investment to $10.50 per share (the original cost basis of your investment, including the sales load).

Table 8.6 *The Three Categories of Expense*

1	2	3
Expense of Entering Fund	**Expenses of Being Invested in Fund**	**Expenses of Exiting Fund**
Sales Load	Management Fee Administrative Fee	Back-End Load Redemption Fee

Table 8.6 shows the costs of mutual fund investing in three basic categories of expense. Let's begin with the first category. As mentioned previously, many (but not all) mutual funds charge investors a fee to purchase shares, referred to as a *front-end load.* This charge compensates the salesperson for reviewing your financial situation and recommending an appropriate mutual fund.

The front-end load is calculated as a percentage of the offering (purchase) price. For instance, if a share has a $10.50 offering price with a 5% load, you are actually paying $10.50 for $9.975 worth of net asset value. This is calculated by subtracting the load of $.525 ($10.50 x 5%) from the $10.50 offering price.

Now let's examine the load as a percentage of the net asset value per share rather than the share's offering price. A load of $.525 per share in our example as a percentage of net asset value (as opposed to the offering price) would not be 5%, but rather 5.26% ($.525 divided by $9.975). Note, therefore, that even though you are actually paying a 5.26% load as a percentage of the amount invested, the mutual fund marketplace calculates the load as a *percentage of the offering price*—which is the net asset value with the load included ($.525 divided by $10.50).

The second category of costs, the cost of being invested in the fund, has two primary components: the *management fee* and the *administrative fee*. The management fee is exclusively for paying the fund manager to manage the fund, and it generally ranges from .50% to 1% of net assets. The administrative fees, on the other hand, are used to pay the transfer agent, custodian fees, director fees, and distribution (marketing and advertising) fees—also known as 12b-1 fees. Sales personnel usually receive part of the 12b-1 fee as annual compensation for having sold the fund originally (12b-1 fees are limited to an annual amount of .75% of net assets, but are typically much lower).

The third category is the cost of exiting or leaving the fund. Many funds charge a fee to exit the fund that is similar to the fee for entering. The charge for leaving the fund is known as a *back-end load* or *contingent deferred sales charge* (CDSC). It is usually charged as a percentage of net asset value with the percentage generally declining over time (typically during the first six years of ownership), and ranging from 6% in year 1 to 1% in year 6. After year 6, no fee is usually assessed for exiting the fund.

In addition to back-end loads, a fund may charge an exiting fee known as a *redemption fee*. This is a flat fee that is assessed against the value of the shares upon selling them.

Various Classes of Load Mutual Fund Shares

Now let's examine the different ways in which these three categories of expenses can be arranged. As you will see, expenses can be arranged in a way that meets both the investor's objectives and the need for the mutual fund company and the salesperson to be adequately compensated.

There are various classes of mutual fund shares, each representing different fund expense structures. (Note that we are discussing *load mutual funds* as opposed to *no-load mutual funds*. Specifically, this means, as we explained earlier, that an up-front sales charge is built into the cost of buying the shares of these funds.) This arrangement allows an investor not only to choose the type of fund (stock, bond, money market, or combination fund) but also to choose a share class (an expense structure) that makes the most sense for the given time frame. Presently, there are four classes of shares: A, B, C, and D shares.

Note, however, that the designation of A, B, C, or D shares is not uniform throughout the industry. For example, one fund's C shares may have the same characteristics as another's B shares. The mutual fund industry is taking steps to clear up these differences, and its goal is eventually to standardize the definitions of the various classes of shares. To that end, the industry will be moving toward the A, B, C, and D share definitions as outlined in Table 8.7.

Table 8.7 *A, B, C, and D Load Shares*

A Shares	B Shares	C Shares	D Shares
Front-End Load	**Back-End Load**	**Level Load**	**Hybrid Level Load**
1. Front-end load 2. Management fee 3. Optional 12b-1 fee 4. No redemption fee or CDSC* 5. Break points offered	1. No front-end load 2. Management fee 3. 12b-1 fee 4. Redemption fee or CDSC 5. Optional conversion to A shares	1. No front-end load 2. Management fee 3. Higher 12b-1 fee 4. No redemption fee or CDSC 5. Optional conversion to A shares	1. Small front-end load 2. Management fee 3. 12b-1 fee 4. Possible redemption fee or CDSC 5. Optional conversion to A shares
Best suited for long time frames and large dollar amounts that can take advantage of break points	Best suited for long time frames and for dollar amounts not large enough to benefit from break points	Best suited when time frame is not long enough to offset front-end or back-end loads	Best suited when time frame is not long enough to offset front-end or back-end loads

**Contingent deferred sales charge*

Front-End Load Shares: A Shares

The first mutual fund class is front-end load shares, or A shares. A shares are principally designed for individuals who are going to invest for the long haul. These shares typically have lower management fees than B shares, optional 12b-1 fees, and no redemption fee or CDSC. The purchase of A shares over B shares is based on the premise that it is more advantageous to pay the load at purchase because it will usually be offset by a lower annual management fee over time. Another consideration with front-end load shares is that they usually offer break points to investors who invest large dollar amounts (the amount varies from fund to fund). Break points are dollar ranges above which the load is either reduced or eliminated.

Back-End Load Shares: B Shares

Back-end load shares, or B shares, are the second mutual fund category. Back-end load shares are the exact opposite of front-end load shares. As we explained earlier in this module, a back-end load is a sales charge applied against the value of a fund when the investor exits the fund (a redemption fee or CDSC). The charge is usually determined as a percentage amount of the assets withdrawn and generally declines over time. For some funds, however, the charge is a percentage of the original purchase amount. B shares usually have back-end charges that range anywhere from 1% to 6% of the funds being withdrawn. These charges eventually decrease to the point where the back-end load vanishes (typically within four to eight years after purchasing the fund). Annual management fees and 12b-1 fees are also charged. Generally speaking, B shares are best suited for investors who don't qualify for break points and plan to invest for periods of time which exceed the period for which the back-end load applies. B shares typically give the shareholder the option to convert the B shares to A shares.

Level-Load Shares: C Shares

Level-load shares, the third category, are generally known as C shares. Unlike front-end load funds or back-end load funds, level-load funds usually do not impose sales charges to either enter or exit the fund (although some level-load funds do charge a small entry or exit fee). These fund companies charge a level-load percentage amount, as opposed to a front- or back-end load, along with the annual management fee. This level load is typically a combination of higher management and 12b-1 fees. C shares are best suited for short-term investors who don't qualify for break points and who will not be investing for a long enough period to offset the expenses of front- or back-end loads. C shares usually provide an option for the shareholder to convert them to A shares.

Hybrid Level-Load Shares: D Shares

The fourth category—hybrid level-load shares, or D shares—typically have a small front-end load and a possible redemption fee or CDSC. Annual management fees and 12b-1 fees are charged. As with the C shares described above, the level load is usually made up of higher management and 12b-1 fees. D shares are most appropriate for short-term investors who don't qualify for break points and who will not be investing for a period that is long enough to compensate for front- or back-end loads. D shares also give the shareholder the option to convert to A shares.

Load versus No-Load Funds

As we explained earlier, mutual funds come in two types: load and no-load. At first glance, you may think that a no-load fund is the better buy since it costs less upfront. However, both load and no-load funds have advantages and disadvantages. The primary advantage of a no-load fund over a load fund is that there is no charge for entering or exiting the fund. As a result, the entire amount invested goes to work for the shareholder. In a load fund, on the other hand, only the net amount after the sales load is invested.

In addition to the load, however, investors must consider the fund's management and administrative fees, along with its past and potential performance. Some load funds, despite their loads and higher expense structures, outperform no-load funds, which makes it worthwhile for the investor to pay the additional expenses. Remember, too, that load charges ensure future sales service by the salesperson.

Investors can find complete details on a mutual fund's expense structure in the fund's prospectus. *Always read the prospectus before investing.*

Choosing Funds

Once you are convinced that mutual funds are for you, you can purchase a fund through (1) a financial planner, (2) a stockbroker or appropriately licensed insurance agent, (3) a discount brokerage firm, or (4) directly from the fund company if it is a no-load fund. Keep in mind that load funds are marketed through sales personnel, which can include discount brokerage firms.

The advantage of using a financial planner, stockbroker, or insurance agent is that they all can help you select the correct fund. Furthermore, if they carry the industry designation of CFP (Certified Financial Planner) or ChFC (Chartered Financial Consultant) it means that they have successfully passed industry testing requirements in the field of financial planning. This better qualifies them to understand your total financial planning needs.

There are also advantages in using a discount brokerage firm. First, discount brokers deal only with many of the leading no-load or low-load funds; this helps narrow the selection process. They also provide prospectuses and other factual mutual fund information. Moreover, they furnish the investor with one consolidated monthly statement, regardless of the number of funds he or she owns.

One drawback is that discount brokerage firms typically charge a .25% fee to the fund company for making the fund available to the public. This charge is directly against the fund's earnings and included in the 12b-1 fee. (Contact discount brokerage firms to find out how to open an account and to get a list of the leading funds the firm makes available.)

If you choose *not* to deal with a financial planner, stockbroker, insurance agent, or discount broker, you can contact a fund company directly to purchase a no-load fund. (Keep in mind that only no-load funds are marketed without sales professionals.) This approach assumes that you will select the fund yourself. The advantage is that you avoid loads and the higher sales and marketing costs associated with load funds. The disadvantage may be that you are not selecting the most appropriate fund based on your specific needs and risk tolerance.

If you go the route of selecting a fund yourself, the best method is to use a rating service or business magazine. There are two primary rating services on the market that track mutual funds: Morningstar Mutual Funds and The Value Line Investment Survey. Both provide one-page descriptions of each fund and track its historical performance against major market indices. Most local public and business libraries carry these rating services. In addition to rating services, many of the leading business magazines (found in libraries and local bookstores) list the top-performing mutual funds by category. The funds in each category are ranked in the order of best to worst, taking risk into account. Also not to be overlooked is the vast amount of mutual fund information made available through computer online services such as America Online, Compuserve and Prodigy. One can also explore the possibilities on the *Internet*.

Minimum Investment Requirements

All funds establish a minimum dollar amount to open an account, and in many cases there are minimum amounts for additional contributions. Most minimum requirements fall between $250 and $1,000, and investors have the option of making payments through payroll deductions or deductions from a checking account. Some funds, although they require a minimum investment amount, allow the investor to pay the amount over the course of a year if the investor will commit to investing the money for a one-year time period and if he or she supports that commitment with an automatic debit payment plan. When buying shares, an investor must also understand the loads (if any), break points (if offered), exchange options available between funds, how to redeem shares (sell shares back to the fund), and at what price a redemption will take place. This information can be found in the prospectus.

Reading the Financial Newspaper

If you are going to invest in mutual funds, you will want to check the price of your shares (net asset value) from time to time, either through the financial newspaper, your brokerage statements, or electronically through your computer. Table 8.8 shows the format in which *The Wall Street Journal* typically presents its mutual fund information in the paper's mutual fund quotation section. Other financial publications follow a similar format. Let's take a look at Table 8.8 now.

Table 8.8 *Mutual Fund Share Prices*

Name	Objective	NAV	Price	Change	YTD	26 WKS	4 YRS
A Bal (p, r, f, t, e, x)	S&B	12.37	13.12	-0.01	2.00	2.70	12.90

Reprinted by permission of The Wall Street Journal, *© 1995 Dow Jones & Company, Inc. All Rights Reserved Worldwide.*

The first column in Table 8.8 is the abbreviated name of the fund. In our example, it is the American Balanced Fund (A Bal), which is found under the fund family name "American Funds" followed by the letters p, r, f, t, e, x. Typically, several funds are listed under the heading for a family of funds.

Here's what the letters after a fund name mean:

- "p" means that the fund charges a 12b-1 fee.
- "r" indicates that the fund has either a contingent deferred sales charge (CDSC) or a redemption fee. (Recall that a CDSC is a back-end sales charge for selling the fund within a certain period of time, and the amount of the charge usually declines over time. The redemption fee, on the other hand, is a fee applied whenever the shares are sold.)
- "f" after the abbreviated name indicates that the fund regularly inputs the previous day's prices instead of the most current day's prices.
- "t" following the name of the fund means it has both a CDSC or redemption fee and a 12b-1 fee.
- "e" indicates that a distribution has been made, which lowers the net asset value.
- "x" means that a dividend has been distributed. (Note that it is better to buy after the distribution or dividend date, if possible, since the distribution or dividend lowers the cost per share and avoids the tax liability created by the distribution.)

These are six of the main letter notations used in the *Journal,* although there are others. Again, if the *Journal* is not used to track mutual fund prices, remember that other financial publications follow a format similar to the one in the table.

The second column in Table 8.8 explains the fund's investment objective–in this case S&B, which stands for stock and bond fund (see *The Wall Street Journal* for a detailed list of objectives). The third column is the net asset value per share (NAV), which is $12.37 as of the close of the previous business day. (The NAV can also be called the bid price, which is the amount you would receive per share if you sold your shares minus a deferred sale charge, if applicable.)

The fourth column is the fund's offering price of $13.12, listed in some newspapers as the buy price or asked price, which is the price you would pay to purchase shares (the NAV plus any applicable sales charges). The fifth column–"Change"–indicates the increase or decrease in the fund's closing price from the previous day. The last three columns report the year-to-date percentage total return (2.00), the percentage total return for the last twenty-six-week period (2.70), and the percentage total return for the most current four-year period (12.90).

Monitoring a Fund

After purchasing a mutual fund, you should monitor the fund's performance. If the fund is tracked by either the Morningstar or Value Line rating services mentioned earlier, note how the fund performs relative to its peers. If the fund is performing poorly on a consistent basis, then you might want to consider switching into a better-performing fund. Also if your goals or financial situation changes, you may choose to select a fund with different risk-return characteristics.

Module 9 Financial Goals, Portfolio Construction and Preparing Financial Statements

Module 9 winds up our book on successful financial planning. This module explores several important topics in which we examine specific concepts that will be useful in creating your own financial plan. Let's begin with the concept of the life cycle and the five potential goals of a financial plan.

The Life Cycle and Five Potential Financial Goals

We do not have forever to save for financial goals. In fact, individuals have to accomplish most of their savings goals during the first two stages of the life cycle: the young adult years–ages 25–44–and the middle years–ages 45–64. The third stage, the elderly years–age 65 and beyond–are typically the retirement years.

While many people begin working in the teenage years, most do not begin earning incomes that will support an individual or family lifestyle until after graduation from college, trade school, or some type of similar vocational training. It is at that point that individuals enter the young adult years. These are the years during which assets accumulate and expenses usually continue to increase (apart from inflation).

The young adult stage is followed by the middle years. Generally, expenses continue to increase but eventually level off during this period. Finally, in the elderly years, expenses typically decline compared to the middle years. However, for some people, expenses actually increase due to an active retirement or, perhaps, higher health care expenses.

Table 9.1 *Financial Goals within the Life Cycle*

Stage 1: Young Adult Years	Stage 2: Middle Years	Stage 3: Elderly Years
1. Emergency Fund 2. Home Down Payment 3. College Costs for Children 4. Saving for Retirement 5. Planned Expenditures	1. Emergency Fund 2. College Costs for Children 3. Saving for Retirement 4. Planned Expenditures	1. Emergency Fund 2. Funding Retirement 3. Planned Expenditures
Age 25 ·················►	45 ·················►	65 ·················►
The Working Years: Ages 25–64		Retirement

Table 9.1 lists the primary financial goals during each of the three life cycles. During stage one, the five primary goals are saving for an emergency fund, a home down payment, college costs for children, retirement, and planned expenditures. During stage two, it is assumed that the home has been purchased. By stage three, it is assumed that the home has been paid off, along with any college costs for children. Let's discuss each of these five goals in detail.

1. Emergency Fund

In a properly designed financial plan, the first goal is to establish an emergency fund. By definition, an emergency fund is three to six months of living costs set aside in a liquid investment to meet any and all kinds of emergencies, including loss of employment. (Note that the loss of earnings due to unemployment may be partially offset by unemployment benefits, depending on the circumstances of employment termination.)

Once an adequate emergency fund is established, then, *and only then,* is it safe to move on to the other goals of a financial plan. This will avoid having to use money invested in other investments to meet the costs of an emergency. Savings set aside for emergency fund purposes should be invested only in money market accounts or interest-bearing checking accounts. This will allow for (1) full accessibility to the funds at all times without loss of principal and (2) interest earnings.

Investments such as certificates of deposit carry penalties for early withdrawal and therefore are inappropriate for an emergency fund. However, if the maturities of the certificates of deposit are staggered in very short time intervals–30-, 60-, and 90-day increments, for example–CDs could act as an alternative method for meeting the liquid investment requirement of an emergency fund.

2. Home Down Payment

The second goal of a financial plan is saving for the down payment on a home. Typically, home down payments range from 10% to 25% of the purchase price, depending on the lender. At the time of purchase there are also closing costs–lender fees, real estate agent fees, and miscellaneous legal and inspection fees–which usually run from 1% to 5% of the purchase price. Keep in mind that after paying the down payment and closing costs, the new homeowner will have to meet the mortgage payments, which consist of principal and interest, real estate taxes on the home, and insurance coverage.

If a short time period, such as one to four years is being used to save for the home down payment, a money market fund, savings account, or certificate of deposit is appropriate. For longer periods of five years and beyond, more aggressive investments can be used–bond and stock mutual funds, for example.

3. College Costs

Assuming that an individual or couple has children, saving for those children's college education is the third goal of a financial plan. Although saving for a college education usually begins after the purchase of a home, it can begin sooner. Again, if the time period in which to save for the cost of college education is short (one to four years), then a money market fund, savings account, or certificates of deposit should be used. If periods of five years or longer are used, more aggressive investments, such as bond and stock mutual funds, are appropriate.

4. Retirement

The fourth goal of a financial plan is retirement. Normally, saving for retirement should start after the purchase of a home; however, it can start earlier. The main drawback of starting a retirement plan too soon is that the funds accumulated may be needed for other reasons. This may present a problem if the funds are invested in a retirement program that does not allow access without penalty; most retirement programs impose penalties if funds are withdrawn before age 59½. Saving for retirement generally involves long time periods and is funded, therefore, with more aggressive investments.

5. Planned Expenditures

The last goal is planned expenditures. Planned expenditures – a new car or an addition to the home, for example – will always be part of a person's financial program. These expenditures should be viewed as ones that are going to occur and will be paid for out of savings rather than by borrowing.

As with the home down payment, if the time period to save for the planned expenditure is from one to four years, then a money market fund, savings account, or certificate of deposit should be used. If, however, the savings period is five years or longer, more aggressive investments may be used.

Compounding Future Costs

In Module 2, "Compounding Inflation," we explained that when utilizing 1949 as the base year for measuring increases in living costs, the first doubling in living costs took place in 1974, the second doubling in 1982, and the third is on its way.

With 1995 as our base year, let's use the cost of a home, the cost of a college education, and the cost of retirement to help clarify the possible increases in future costs. Let's assume that the cost of a new home in 1995 is $150,000, the cost of a four-year public college education for two children is $75,000 ($37,500 each), and the amount required to fund retirement for a 20-year period is $1 million. Table 9.2 shows us what these costs will increase to in the years 2000, 2005, 2010, and 2015 using a 4% average inflation rate. (Note that although the cost of a home, college education, and retirement all increase by the same rate of inflation in this example, this is not normally the case.)

Table 9.2 *Future Costs*

Year 1995	Home $150,000	College Education $75,000	Retirement $1,000,000
2000	$182,498	$91,249	$1,216,653
2005	$222,037	$111,018	$1,480,244
2010	$270,142	$135,070	$1,800,943
2015	$328,669	$164,333	$2,191,123

As you can see in Table 9.2, a home that costs $150,000 in 1995 will cost $182,498 by the year 2000. The future costs to purchase that same home will continue to increase at a compound rate based on the 4% rate of inflation. By the year 2015, the cost of that home will be $328,669, more than double its cost in 1995. Similarly, in this scenario, the costs of college education and retirement will both more than double during 1995 to 2015. College education costs will increase from $75,000 to $164,333; the cost of retirement will rise from $1 million to $2,191,123.

Viewing a Home as an Investment

It is important to note that the longer you wait to purchase a home, the more it will increase in cost because of the effect of inflation. Furthermore, given the order of priority we've established for the five primary financial goals in our financial planning system, the longer you wait to buy a home, the more it can delay saving for your children's college education and your retirement.

In a best-case scenario, a house can be purchased with cash–that is, no money is borrowed to make the purchase. In actuality, however, most individuals do not have adequate savings to purchase a home for cash. As a result, buying a home usually includes a down payment amount and a mortgage amount that represents the difference between the purchase price and the down payment. Now let's see how borrowing to purchase a home can be positive.

Assume that we want to purchase a home that costs $100,000 with a 25% down payment ($25,000). Our $25,000 investment (down payment), along with the $75,000 mortgage amount, will therefore control an asset valued at $100,000 (not factoring in closing costs).

If housing inflation is 5% during the next five-year period, the value of the home will increase from $100,000 to $127,628. This appreciation in asset value represents a total compound increase of 27.63%.

From an investment standpoint, we did not contribute $100,000 to purchase the home, but rather only $25,000. We borrowed the other $75,000. Using borrowed dollars to purchase an asset is called *leverage*. The ability to purchase an asset with borrowed funds means that the entire value of the asset will appreciate in value while the amount borrowed will remain fixed.

In our example, therefore, at the end of the five-year period, the $25,000 cash outlay yields a pretax increase in real estate value of $27,628 (from the $100,000 purchase price to the $127,628 current asset value). This represents a 111% return on the cash down payment (27,628 ÷ 25,000). You'll note that these calculations do not factor in the interest costs on the borrowed money, the closing costs to buy the home, and the costs of owning the home (taxes and insurance).

Thus, in the case of a home or other real estate, borrowing can allow for appreciation in the total value of the property–definitely a positive use of leverage (borrowing). There are also negative examples. For instance, when a car is financed, its value depreciates over time (note this depreciation will occur whether or not the car is financed). As a result, there is no appreciation in the value of the asset to offset the financing costs.

Choosing the Most Suitable Mortgage Term

If you can afford it, a fifteen-year mortgage term is preferable to a thirty-year mortgage when purchasing a home. Although a fifteen-year mortgage will have a higher monthly payment than a thirty-year mortgage, there will also be a considerable savings in interest costs because of the shorter mortgage term.

For example, a $100,000 mortgage at 8% interest for a thirty-year period requires a monthly payment of $733.76. A fifteen-year mortgage at the same rate requires a monthly payment amount of $955.65. If you could meet the additional payment of $221.89 per month, not only could you pay the mortgage off fifteen years sooner, but you would also save *$92,137* in interest costs (the difference between the total cash outlay for a thirty-year mortgage of $264,154 and a fifteen-year mortgage of $172,017). This savings arises from accelerating the loan payment schedule. The offset to this is that interest costs will not be available as a deduction for income tax purposes for as long a period of time.

However, because the fifteen-year mortgage will be paid off fifteen years sooner than a thirty-year mortgage, the savings can be used for other financial goals, such as college costs for children or retirement. If you already have a thirty-year mortgage, making an extra principal payment every month will help pay down the mortgage faster. You can work out an accelerated pay-down schedule with your lender (bank or savings and loan institution) to determine how much you could save by paying off your mortgage sooner.

Delaying Financial Goals (Domino Effect)

In the beginning of this module we discussed how continuing inflation will drive up the cost of the primary goals of a financial plan. Because we live in a world of compounding inflation, the costs of a home, college education, and retirement continue to increase annually.

As a result, future costs are not static but escalating. Therefore, any delay in funding one of your financial goals can delay the funding of a second financial goal, and so on. This could result in less available time overall for you to fund some of your financial goals. Furthermore, as investment time frames are shortened, there is less time in which to earn an investment return, which in turn requires you to save more annually to reach a financial goal. This could be further complicated if the performance of an investment is unfavorable.

Table 9.3 summarizes why delaying any financial goal is costly–especially the delay of buying a home since it has an impact on the remaining goals. Keep in mind that once you purchase a home, assuming the mortgage payment is fixed, the housing portion of living costs remains constant (except for real estate taxes and insurance costs, which are subject to periodic increases). This gives you the opportunity to increase savings as your income increases.

Table 9.3 *Delaying Financial Goals*

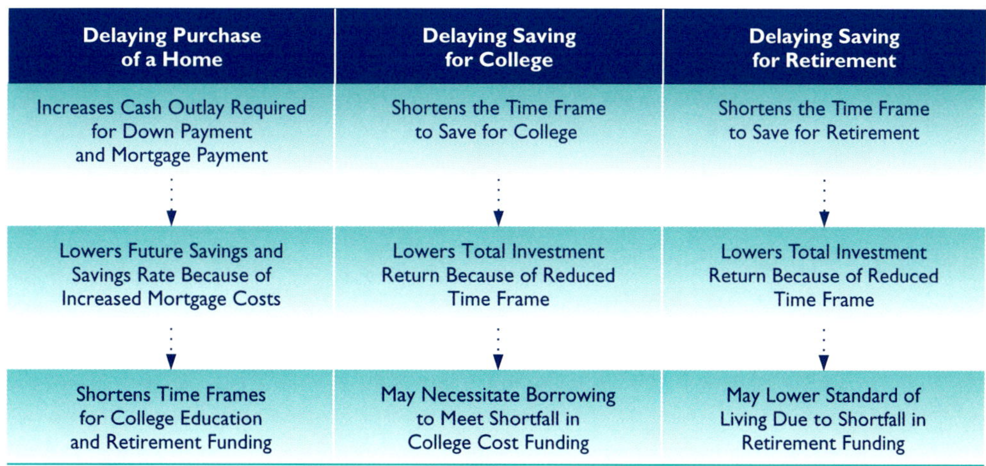

Delaying Purchase of a Home	Delaying Saving for College	Delaying Saving for Retirement
Increases Cash Outlay Required for Down Payment and Mortgage Payment	Shortens the Time Frame to Save for College	Shortens the Time Frame to Save for Retirement
↓	↓	↓
Lowers Future Savings and Savings Rate Because of Increased Mortgage Costs	Lowers Total Investment Return Because of Reduced Time Frame	Lowers Total Investment Return Because of Reduced Time Frame
↓	↓	↓
Shortens Time Frames for College Education and Retirement Funding	May Necessitate Borrowing to Meet Shortfall in College Cost Funding	May Lower Standard of Living Due to Shortfall in Retirement Funding

Dollar Cost Averaging

It is a fact that most investors invest periodically rather than on a one-time basis. This periodic investment approach, which is known as *dollar cost averaging,* can take place monthly, quarterly, annually, or during any period of time the investor selects.

Table 9.4 *Dollar Cost Averaging (1964-1973)*

A	B	C	D	E	F	G
Year	**Amount Invested**	**Purchase Price**	**Shares Purchased**	**Cumulative Shares**	**Total Invested**	**Current Value**
		$10.00				
1964	$ 1,000	11.65	85.84	85.84	$ 1,000	$ 1,000
1965	1,000	13.10	76.34	162.18	2,000	2,125
1966	1,000	11.78	84.89	247.07	3,000	2,910
1967	1,000	14.60	68.49	315.56	4,000	4,607
1968	1,000	16.21	61.69	377.25	5,000	6,115
1969	1,000	14.83	67.43	444.68	6,000	6,595
1970	1,000	15.42	64.85	509.53	7,000	7,857
1971	1,000	17.63	56.72	566.25	8,000	9,983
1972	1,000	20.98	47.66	613.91	9,000	12,880
1973	1,000	17.90	55.87	669.78	10,000	**$11,989**
Total	**$10,000**	$15.41				

The average cost per share is $15.41 (bottom column C).
Source for S&P Data: © Stocks, Bonds, Bills, and Inflation 1995 Yearbook™, *Ibbotson Associates, Chicago (annually updates work by Roger G. Ibbotson and Rex A. Sinquefield). Used with permission. All rights reserved.*

Table 9.4 illustrates the results of investing $1,000 at the end of each year during the ten-year period from 1964 to 1973. In this example, we start with the $10 share price of a hypothetical mutual fund that thereafter increases or decreases, based on the total returns of large company stocks as measured by the S&P 500. Therefore, the table illustrates not only dollar cost averaging, but also how you would have fared if you were dollar cost averaging annually into a large company stock mutual fund from 1964 to 1973.

As you can see from the data in column C, the share purchase price at the end of each year varies. The purchase price represents the net asset value per share at the end of each year; no distributions are being made from the earnings of the fund. As a result, fund earn ings or losses increase or decrease the share price and therefore the number of shares purchased each year (column D, which is column B divided by column C). Column E indicates the cumulative number of shares, column F shows the total amount invested, and column G reports the total portfolio value (column C multiplied by column E).

At the end of the period, the current value of the shares owned is $11,989 (column G). The total amount invested is $10,000. Therefore, the increase in value is $1,989, an average return of 3.97% per year based on the periodic investment approach utilized in Table 9.4. Although this paints a poor total return picture for stock market investing during those ten years, let's see what the return would have been if you had invested during the next ten-year period (1974–1983) using a $1,000 annual end-of-year dollar cost averaging approach.

Table 9.5 *Dollar Cost Averaging (1974-1983)*

A	B	C	D	E	F	G
Year	**Amount Invested**	**Purchase Price**	**Shares Purchased**	**Cumulative Shares**	**Total Invested**	**Current Value**
		$10.00				
1974	$ 1,000	7.35	136.05	136.05	$ 1,000	$ 1,000
1975	1,000	10.08	99.21	235.26	2,000	2,371
1976	1,000	12.48	80.13	315.39	3,000	3,936
1977	1,000	11.58	86.36	401.75	4,000	4,652
1978	1,000	12.34	81.04	482.79	5,000	5,958
1979	1,000	14.62	68.40	551.19	6,000	8,058
1980	1,000	19.36	51.65	602.84	7,000	11,671
1981	1,000	18.41	54.32	657.16	8,000	12,098
1982	1,000	22.35	44.74	701.90	9,000	15,687
1983	1,000	27.38	36.52	738.42	10,000	**$20,218**
Total	**$10,000**	$15.60				

The average cost per share is $15.60 (bottom column C).
Source for S&P Data: © Stocks, Bonds, Bills, and Inflation 1995 Yearbook™, *Ibbotson Associates, Chicago (annually updates work by Roger G. Ibbotson and Rex A. Sinquefield). Used with permission. All rights reserved.*

As Table 9.5 shows, at the end of the period, the current value of the shares owned is $20,218. The total amount invested is $10,000. Therefore, the increase in value using the periodic investment approach is $10,218, an average return of 14.91% per year.

Table 9.4 (which covers the years 1964–1973) reflects a period that began with the last two years of a long-term bull market (that actually started in 1949 and ended in 1965). The remaining eight years were largely a bear market for large company stocks. Table 9.5, on the other hand, covers the years 1974–1983 and begins during a bear market for the first eight years in large company stocks and ends at the start of a bull market (which began in 1982). (Note: In an effort not to exaggerate total returns, we did not illustrate dollar cost averaging into large company stocks during bull market cycles, such as occurred during the bull market of 1949–1965 or that began in 1982 and continued through 1994.)

In summary, dollar cost averaging can produce interim results that vary depending on the direction of the financial markets. Over the long run, however, since the stock market has increased (see Module 7) dollar cost averaging remains an effective method for investing.

Time Value of Money

Understanding the time value of money is essential in choosing any type of investment to fund a financial goal. The time value of money is based on the concept that having a dollar now (today) is worth more than having it at some point in the future (forget about inflation for the moment.) This is because you can invest a dollar that you have today and earn an investment return.

For instance, if you invest $1 today earning a 6% annual rate of return, at the end of one year, the investment will increase to $1.06. In this example the value today (the present value) is $1 and the value one year from now (the future value) is $1.06. If you had the choice, therefore, it would be better to receive $1 now rather than $1 a year from now since receiving it today would allow you to invest the dollar and earn interest on it throughout the year.

The cost of not receiving the $1 now and thereby forgoing the interest that you could have earned is called *opportunity cost*. As a rule, the higher the potential rate of return, the greater the opportunity cost.

Risk and Return

Now that we have briefly examined the concept behind the time value of money, let's talk about investing. As we explained in Module 7, as we venture into riskier types of investments, there is the potential for greater returns. This is the risk and return tradeoff.

In Module 7, we discussed the inflation-adjusted returns for the cash investments market, the long-term corporate bond market, and the stock market for large and small company stocks. Table 9.6 illustrates the non-inflation-adjusted total, average, and range of returns for these markets and, in addition, the long-term tax-exempt bond market.

Table 9.6 *Non-Inflation-Adjusted Range of Returns 1949-1994*

Period 1949–1994	Cash Investments	Long-Term Tax-Exempt Bond Market	Long-Term Corporate Bond Market	Large Company Stocks	Small Company Stocks
Total Return	869%	419%	1154%	19845%	54338%
Average Return	5.10%	3.60%	5.70%	12.20%	14.70%
Range of Returns	1% to 15%	-18% to 48%	-8% to 43%	-26% to 53%	-31% to 84%
	Risk and Return Increase ►				

Source: © Stocks, Bonds, Bills, and Inflation 1995 Yearbook™, *Ibbotson Associates, Chicago (annually updates work by Roger G. Ibbotson and Rex A. Sinquefield). Used with permission. All rights reserved.*

As you can see in Table 9.6, the returns increase as you move from cash investments to stock investments. However, so does the risk. This increased risk is measured by the investment's increased volatility (the high and low ranges around the average). As the table illustrates, moving into the riskier categories widens the range of returns, in both positive *and* negative directions.

For example, small company stocks, which provide the greatest rates of return, also provide the greatest losses: The greatest annual return in one year for small company stocks was 84%, the largest loss was -31%. If an investor had $100,000 invested in small company stocks during a year when there was a 31% decrease, the value of the stocks would decrease to $69,000. (Keep in mind that the ranges of returns in Table 9.6 were derived from market indexes; returns for cash investments were based on a portfolio consisting of one 30-day Treasury bill. Therefore, the investment you have could perform better or worse than the averages presented in the table.)

As a final point, looking at the average rates of return for this forty-six-year period, it is interesting to note that long-term corporate bonds did not perform significantly better than cash investments. This is primarily because cash investments, although they offer lower returns, are also free from negative returns.

Volatility of the Financial Markets

One of the most important investment decisions you'll have to make is determining the level of risk you are willing to take. While all investors want the large returns offered from the stock and bond markets, most are unaware of the risk that goes with attaining these longer-term returns.

When investing in a money market account or an interest-bearing checking account, you usually will have minimal risk of losing any of your principal—that is, interest is earned on the invested funds each year while the underlying principal amount remains secure. However, when searching for higher returns by investing in the bond and stock market, you must understand that in certain years the underlying principal amount invested can, in fact, decline. This can thwart unprepared investors and divert them from their long-term financial goals.

Take a look at Tables 9.7, 9.8, 9.9, and 9.10. Table 9.7 shows the negative non-inflation-adjusted total returns for long-term tax-exempt bonds. Table 9.8 presents the negative non-inflation-adjusted total returns for long-term corporate bonds. Table 9.9 tracks the negative non-inflation-adjusted total returns for large company stocks. Table 9.10 illustrates the negative non-inflation-adjusted total returns for small company stocks. (Note: Because all returns were calculated for the period 1949–1994 using market indexes, investors in each of these market segments could have actually experienced results better or worse than those presented in the four tables.)

Table 9.7 *Years in Which Negative Non-Inflation-Adjusted Total Returns Occurred for Long-Term Tax-Exempt Bonds (1949–1994)*

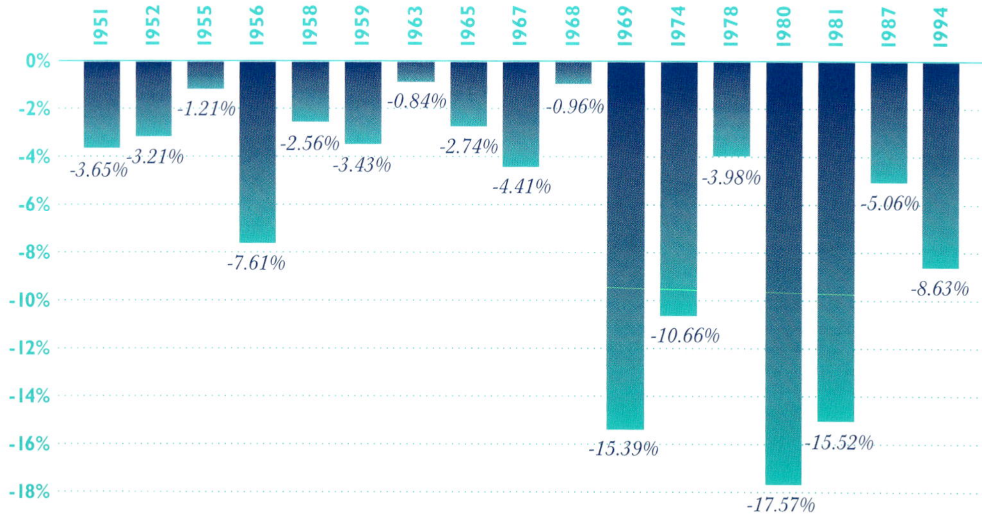

Source: © Stocks, Bonds, Bills, and Inflation 1995 Yearbook™, *Ibbotson Associates, Chicago (annually updates work by Roger G. Ibbotson and Rex A. Sinquefield). Used with permission. All rights reserved.*

As Table 9.7 illustrates, there were seventeen years in which the long-term tax-exempt bond market experienced negative returns during the period 1949–1994. The largest loss occurred in 1980 (-17.57%), and the smallest occurred in 1963 (-.84%).

Table 9.8 *Years in Which Negative Non-Inflation-Adjusted Total Returns Occurred for Long-Term Corporate Bonds (1949–1994)*

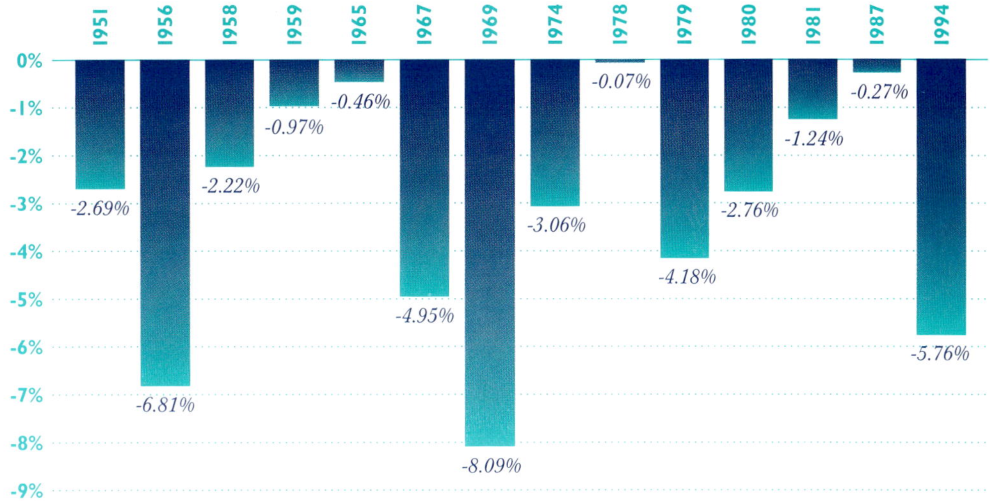

Source: © Stocks, Bonds, Bills, and Inflation 1995 Yearbook™, *Ibbotson Associates, Chicago (annually updates work by Roger G. Ibbotson and Rex A. Sinquefield). Used with permission. All rights reserved.*

There were fourteen years in which the long-term corporate bond market experienced negative returns during the same time period as shown in Table 9.7. The largest loss occurred in 1969 (-8.09%), and the smallest occurred in 1978 (-.07%).

Table 9.9 *Years in Which Negative Non-Inflation-Adjusted Total Returns Occurred for Large Company Stocks (1949–1994)*

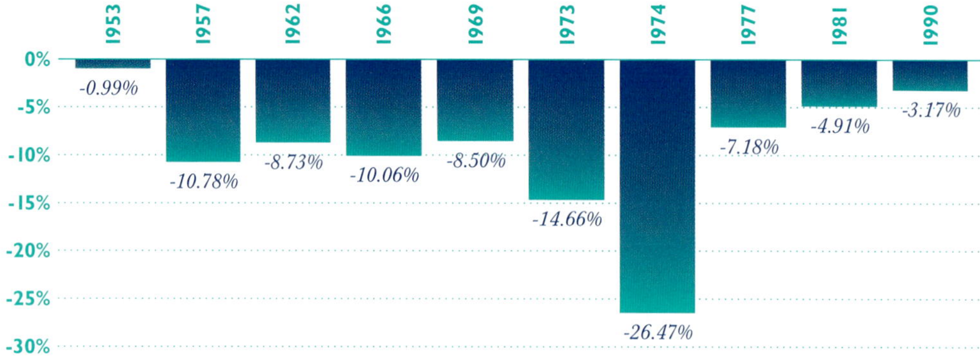

Source: © Stocks, Bonds, Bills, and Inflation 1995 Yearbook™, *Ibbotson Associates, Chicago (annually updates work by Roger G. Ibbotson and Rex A. Sinquefield). Used with permission.*

In the large company stock market, there were ten years of negative returns during the period 1949–1994, (see Table 9.9). The largest loss was in 1974 (-26.47%); the smallest loss was in 1953 (-.99%).

Table 9.10 *Years in Which Negative Non-Inflation-Adjusted Total Returns Occurred for Small Company Stocks (1949–1994)*

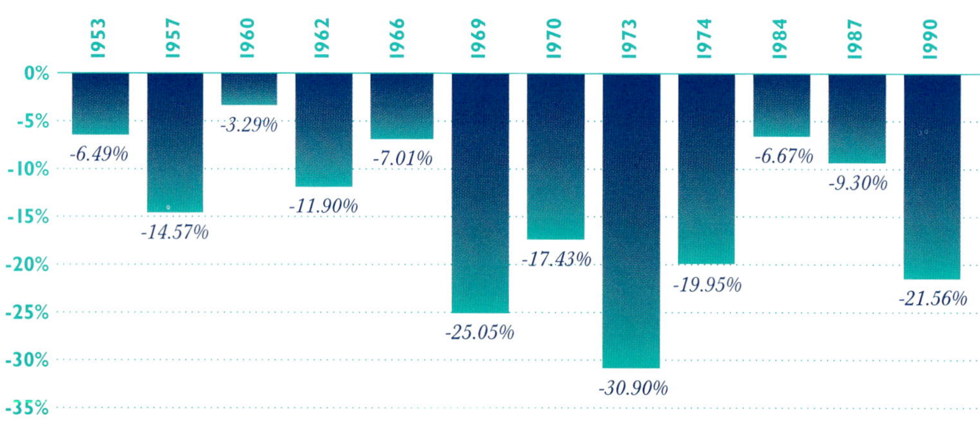

Source: © Stocks, Bonds, Bills, and Inflation 1995 Yearbook™, *Ibbotson Associates, Chicago (annually updates work by Roger G. Ibbotson and Rex A. Sinquefield). Used with permission.*

As Table 9.10 illustrates, during the same 1949–1994 period, there were 12 years in which the small company stock market had negative returns. The largest losses occurred in 1969 (-30.90%), the smallest in 1960 (-3.29%).

Stock Market Declines

The years 1973 and 1974, a time when it was feared the supply of oil from the oil-producing export countries (OPEC) to the United States would be cut off, go on record as the two worst back-to-back years of stock market declines in the post-World War II era.

If you had $100,000 invested in large company stocks at the beginning of 1973, the investment would have declined $37,249 in value to $62,751 by the end of 1974 (as measured by the S&P 500). This compound loss in value most likely would have driven the typical investor out of the stock market completely, probably to seek shelter in the safety of money market accounts or interest-bearing checking accounts. It would have taken an investor with a tremendous amount of confidence in the financial markets to remain invested during this period of time.

The point of this discussion is not to frighten you away from the stock market. Quite the opposite. Its purpose is to foster your understanding of the realities of stock (and bond) market investing. (Even though the bond market did not share losses of the same magnitude as the stock market, there were still double-digit losses in the *long-term tax-exempt* bond market.) What is essential for you to understand is that despite market downturns, the stock market has been *increasing over the long run* and most likely will continue to do so. Nevertheless, there is always the possibility of painful down markets (bear market cycles), which are a part of being invested in the financial markets. The good news is that all bear market cycles in the past have been followed by positive up markets (bull market cycles). It is up to you to determine what risks you as an investor can or cannot tolerate.

Cash Investments

We should mention here that cash investments do not suffer percentage declines because the investment vehicles supporting cash investments are very short-term in nature and usually reach maturity in ninety days. If there is an adverse change in interest rates, which affects the underlying investments used in a money market or savings account, the investments are simply held to maturity. This avoids a loss in the principal amount invested.

Staying Invested during Down Markets

Although staying invested during down markets is difficult, selling out and deciding when to get back in can be even worse. Analyzing the financial markets using a long-term perspective teaches us that the longer an investor stays invested, the more the positive rates of return tend to offset the negative rates of return. Tables 9.11 and 9.12 show the non-inflation-adjusted range of returns for 5-, 10-, 15-, and 20-year holding periods for long-term corporate bonds and large company stocks, beginning in 1949 and ending in 1994.

The data presented in Tables 9.11 and 9.12 are based on rolling averages for each 5-, 10-, 15-, and 20-year holding period during the overall timespan from 1949 to 1994. For example, the data for a 5-year holding period are based on the rolling averages for each of the 5-year periods within the total timespan (1949–1953, 1950–1954, 1951–1955, and so on through 1990–1994).The "High" and "Low" rates represent the highest and lowest rate of return an investment in long-term corporate bonds or large company stocks experienced during each of the rolling five-year periods from 1949–1994. The average rate of return for the rolling five-year periods from 1949–1994 was calculated by averaging the data for each of the five-year periods within the overall timeframe. This same approach applies to the 10-, 15-, and 20-year rolling periods.

One can learn a valuable lesson by studying these tables: As you increase the length of time your money is invested, you decrease the likelihood of loss. At the same time, the range of returns (the highs and lows) becomes narrower as the lower-return years are averaged in with the high-return years.

Table 9.11 *Non-Inflation-Adjusted Range of Returns for Long-Term Corporate Bonds 1949–1994*

Source: © Stocks, Bonds, Bills, and Inflation 1995 Yearbook™, *Ibbotson Associates, Chicago (annually updates work by Roger G. Ibbotson and Rex A. Sinquefield). Used with permission. All rights reserved.*

Table 9.11 illustrates the high, low, and average non-inflation-adjusted returns for long-term corporate bonds during 5-, 10-, 15-, and 20-year holding periods. Holding periods of under five years typically do not allow enough time to react to and counter significant losses should they occur. For the 5-year holding period, the high is 22.51%, the low is -2.22%, and the average is 6%. When the investment is extended to ten years, the high is 16.32%, the low is 1% and the average is 5.90%. For a 15-year holding period, the high is 11.57%, the low is 1.02%, and the average is 5.50%. For a 20-year holding period, the high is 10.16%, the low is 1.34%, and the average is 5.36%. Note how volatility (the range between the highs and lows) decreased the longer the investment period, even though the average return for each holding period remained relatively constant (from 6% in the 5-year holding period down only to 5.36% in the 20-year period.)

Table 9.12 *Non-Inflation-Adjusted Range of Returns for Large Company Stocks 1949–1994*

25%
20%
15%
10%
5%
0%
-5%

	5-Year	10-Year	15-Year	20-Year
High	23.92	20.06	16.61	14.92
Average	12.08	11.39	10.61	9.94
Low	-2.36	1.24	4.31	6.53

Source: © Stocks, Bonds, Bills, and Inflation 1995 Yearbook™, *Ibbotson Associates, Chicago (annually updates work by Roger G. Ibbotson and Rex A. Sinquefield). Used with permission. All rights reserved.*

Table 9.12 shows the high, low, and average non-inflation-adjusted returns for large company stocks. For the 5-year holding period, the high is 23.92%, the low is -2.36%, and the average is 12.08%. For ten years, the high is 20.06%, the low is 1.24%, and the average is 11.39%. For a 15-year holding period, the high is 16.61%, the low is 4.31%, and the average is 10.61%. And for a 20-year period, the high is 14.92%, the low is 6.53%, and the average is 9.94%. Averages ranged from 9.94% to 12.08%—again, relatively constant.

Asset Allocation

As we explained earlier, investing in the financial markets involves risk. The least risky market is the cash investments market, and the most risky is the small company stock market. The middle of the road is the bond market.

While investors who invest only in cash investments may never lose any money, their total returns over the long run will be substantially lower than bond and stock market returns. One way to achieve a good risk-return blend is to divide your portfolio among the stock market, the bond market, and the cash investments market. This process is called *asset allocation*.

The idea behind asset allocation is that diversification among different markets reduces overall risk. For instance, if your portfolio is diversified among large and small company stocks, long-term corporate bonds, and cash investments, percentage declines in any one market might be offset by percentage increases in another market. Over the long run, this tends to smooth out portfolio return (reducing the highs and lows) by blending the returns of all three markets. Like the tortoise in the fable, slow and steady wins the race. The following are four examples of asset allocations, starting with a conservative allocation and ending with a highly aggressive allocation.

Table 9.13 *(1) Conservative Asset Allocation*

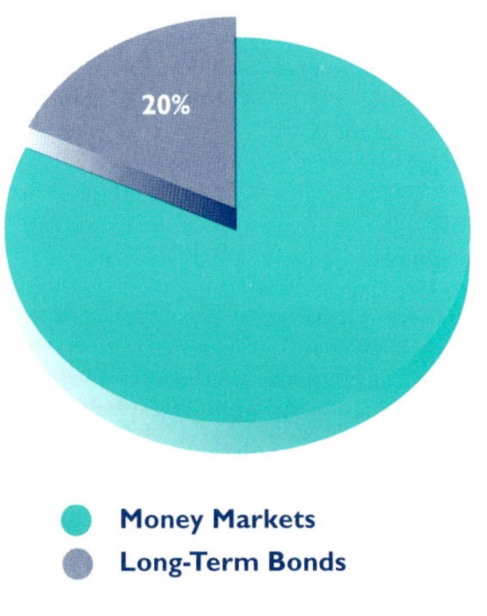

Money Markets
Long-Term Bonds

Table 9.14 *(2) Moderate Risk Asset Allocation*

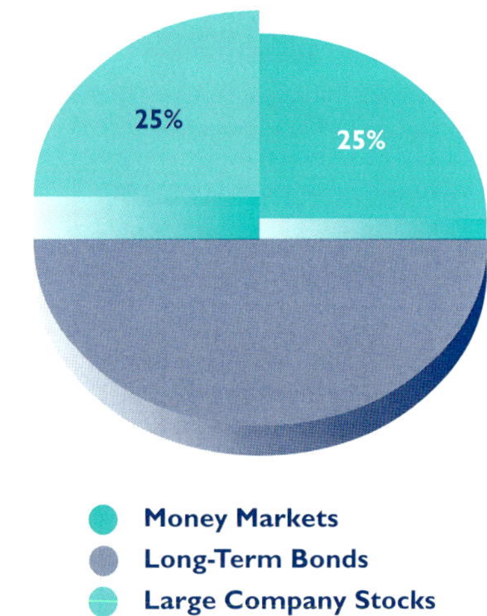

Money Markets
Long-Term Bonds
Large Company Stocks

Table 9.15 *(3) Aggressive Asset Allocation*

Table 9.16 *(4) Highly Aggressive Asset Allocation*

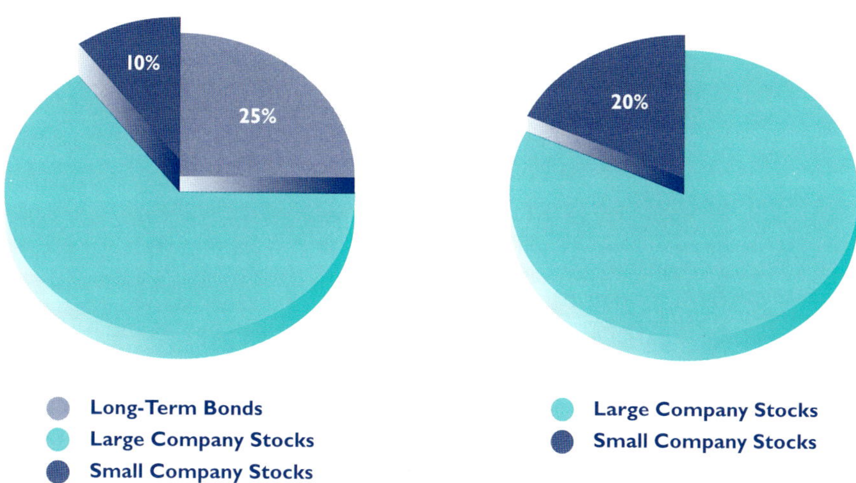

Let's take a look at the non-inflation-adjusted returns an investor would have realized over the forty-six-year period from 1949 through 1994 using the four different asset allocations. Total returns will be illustrated for 5-, 10-, 15-, and 20-year holding periods.

Table 9.17 *Conservative Asset Allocation: 80% Money Markets, 20% Long-Term Bonds*

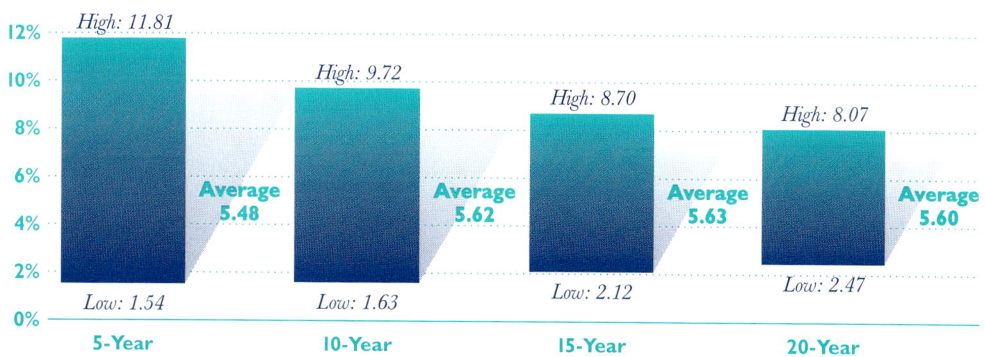

Source: © Stocks, Bonds, Bills, and Inflation 1995 Yearbook™, *Ibbotson Associates, Chicago (annually updates work by Roger G. Ibbotson and Rex A. Sinquefield). Used with permission. All rights reserved. Rebalanced every 5 years.*

Table 9.17 shows the total non-inflation-adjusted returns using a conservative asset allocation of 80% money markets and 20% long-term bonds. For a five-year holding period, the high is 11.81%; the low is 1.54%. For a ten-year holding period, the high is 9.72%; the low is 1.63%. For fifteen years, the high is 8.70%; the low is 2.12%. For twenty years, the high is 8.07%; the low is 2.47%. As we explained earlier (and this table illustrates), volatility decreases as the investment time frame increases. Average returns ranged between 5.48% and 5.63%.

Table 9.18 *Moderate Risk Asset Allocation: 25% Money Markets, 50% Long-Term Bonds, 25% Large Company Stocks*

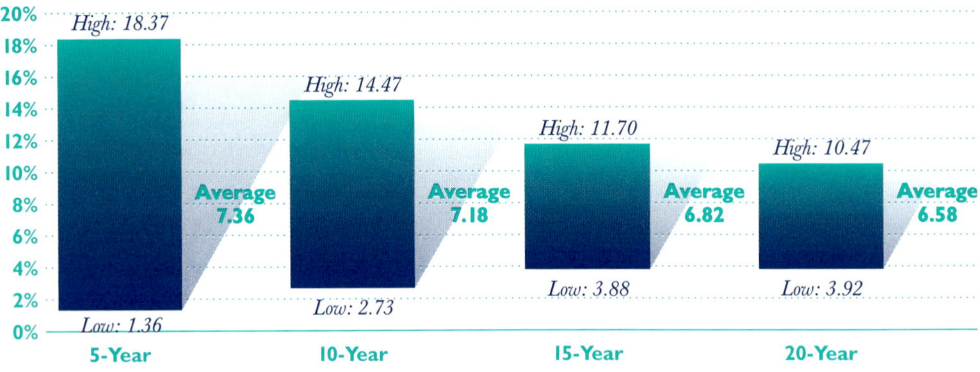

Source: © Stocks, Bonds, Bills, and Inflation 1995 Yearbook™, *Ibbotson Associates, Chicago (annually updates work by Roger G. Ibbotson and Rex A. Sinquefield). Used with permission. All rights reserved. Rebalanced every 10 years.*

Table 9.18 indicates the total non-inflation-adjusted returns using an asset allocation of 25% money markets, 50% long-term bonds, and 25% large company stocks – a moderate risk allocation. For a five-year holding period, the high is 18.37%; the low is 1.36%. For a ten-year period, the high is 14.47%; the low is 2.73%. For fifteen years, the high is 11.70%; the low is 3.88%. For twenty years, the high is 10.47%; the low is 3.92%. Again, as the investment time frames increase, the ranges between the highs and the lows decrease. Average returns ranged from 6.58% to 7.36%.

Table 9.19 *Aggressive Asset Allocation: 25% Long-Term Bonds, 65% Large Company Stocks, 10% Small Company Stocks*

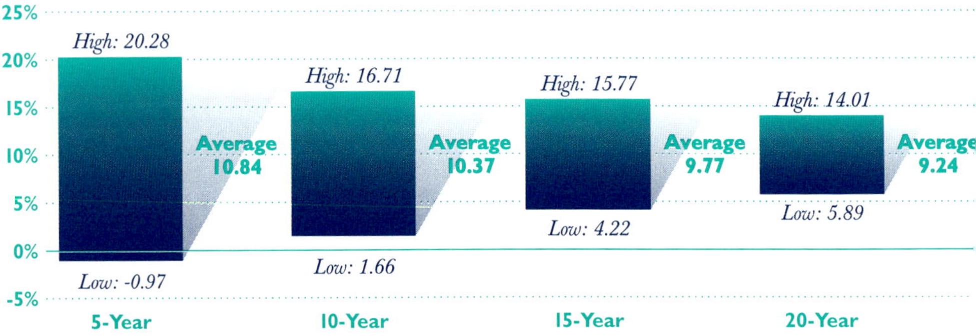

Source: © Stocks, Bonds, Bills, and Inflation 1995 Yearbook™, *Ibbotson Associates, Chicago (annually updates work by Roger G. Ibbotson and Rex A. Sinquefield). Used with permission. All rights reserved. Rebalanced every 15 years.*

Table 9.19 illustrates the total non-inflation-adjusted returns using an aggressive asset allocation of 25% long-term bonds, 65% large company stocks, and 10% small company stocks. The high is 20.28%; the low -0.97% for a five-year holding period. The high is 16.71%; the low is 1.66% for a ten-year period. For fifteen years, the high is 15.77%; the low is 4.22%. For a twenty-year period, the high is 14.01%; the low is 5.89%. Average returns were from 9.24% to 10.84%, with the range between highs and lows narrowing as the investment period lengthened.

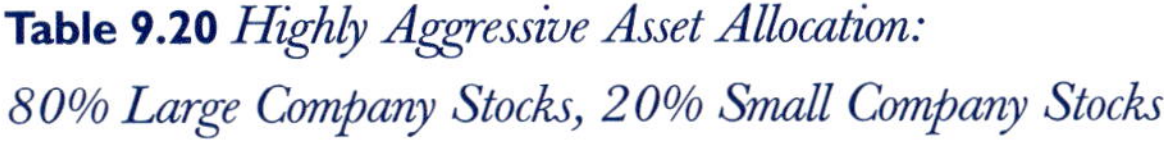

Table 9.20 *Highly Aggressive Asset Allocation: 80% Large Company Stocks, 20% Small Company Stocks*

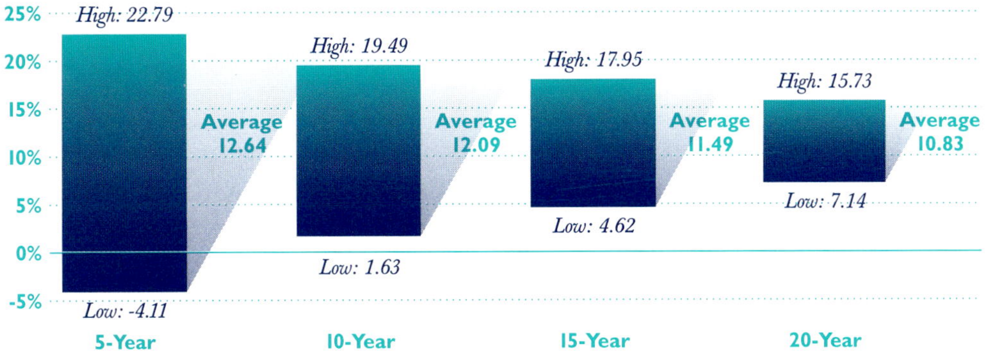

Source: © Stocks, Bonds, Bills, and Inflation 1995 Yearbook™, *Ibbotson Associates, Chicago (annually updates work by Roger G. Ibbotson and Rex A. Sinquefield). Used with permission. All rights reserved. Rebalanced every 20 years.*

Table 9.20 illustrates once more that the longer the investment, the smaller the difference between high and low returns – this time for a highly aggressive asset allocation of 80% large company stocks and 20% small company stocks. For a five-year holding period, the high is 22.79%; the low is -4.11%. For a ten-year period, the high is 19.49%; the low is 1.63%. For fifteen years, the high is 17.95%; the low is 4.62%. For twenty years, the high is 15.73%; the low is 7.14%. The average return ranged from 10.83% to 12.64%.

By defining your financial goals, and deciding on your tolerance for risk, you can select an asset allocation formula that works best for your particular circumstances.

Discount Brokerage Firms

Asset allocation can be carried out very efficiently by using a variety of the stock, bond, and money market mutual funds offered through discount brokerage firms. The reason we mention a discount brokerage firm here is that it provides one consolidated statement at the end of each month for all the different funds you own, which makes tracking your various funds easy and accurate. There is usually some type of fee for this service, but it is charged by the discount broker to the fund company and typically applied against the earnings of the fund, rather than charged directly to the customer. Some of the leading discount brokerage firms have asset allocation software available for interested investors.

Following is a summary of the non-inflation-adjusted returns for 5-, 10-, 15-, and 20-year holding periods using the various asset allocations just presented in Tables 9.17 through 9.20. As you review the return data shown, keep in mind the asset classes are money markets, long-term bonds, large company stocks, and finally, small company stocks.

Table 9.21 *Summary of Asset Allocation Portfolio Returns*

Risk		Time ··········►			
Low	**Conservative Asset Allocation**	**5-Year Period**	**10-Year Period**	**15-Year Period**	**20-Year Period**
	80% Money Markets, 20% Long-Term Bonds				
	High	11.81%	9.72%	8.70%	8.07%
	Average	5.48	5.62	5.63	5.60
	Low	1.54	1.63	2.12	2.47
	Moderate Risk Asset Allocation	**5-Year Period**	**10-Year Period**	**15-Year Period**	**20-Year Period**
	25% Money Markets, 50% Long-Term Bonds, 25% Large Stocks				
	High	18.37%	14.47%	11.70%	10.47%
	Average	7.36	7.18	6.82	6.58
	Low	1.36	2.73	3.88	3.92
	Aggressive Asset Allocation	**5-Year Period**	**10-Year Period**	**15-Year Period**	**20-Year Period**
	25% Long-Term Bonds, 65% Large Stocks, 10% Small Stocks				
	High	20.28%	16.71%	15.77%	14.01%
	Average	10.84	10.37	9.77	9.24
	Low	-0.97	1.66	4.22	5.89
	Highly Aggressive Asset Allocation	**5-Year Period**	**10-Year Period**	**15-Year Period**	**20-Year Period**
	80% Large Stocks, 20% Small Stocks				
	High	22.79%	19.49%	17.95%	15.73%
▼	Average	12.64	12.09	11.49	10.83
High	Low	-4.11	1.63	4.62	7.14

Source: © Stocks, Bonds, Bills, and Inflation 1995 Yearbook™, *Ibbotson Associates, Chicago (annually updates work by Roger G. Ibbotson and Rex A. Sinquefield). Used with permission.*

Choosing Safer Investments as You Approach a Goal

As you approach a particular financial goal, you may want to begin moving a portion, if not all, of the funds you have invested in a stock or bond fund into a less risky investment. For example, if you have been saving for your children's college education for the past eight years using a stock mutual fund and you will need to access the money in year ten, you may want to transfer some of the funds into cash investments before then. We recommend you consider this technique since downturns in the stock and bond markets *do* occur, as we pointed out earlier. When a large amount of money is invested, these percentage losses can translate into significant dollar amounts. Moving portions (or all) of your stock or bond investment into the safe harbor of cash investments as you near your financial goal protects you against the possibility that a market downturn would erode your principal in the year you need the funds. Conversely, moving your investments into cash instruments during these years when the principal is highest could also cause you to miss out on potential large returns if the stock or bond markets are particularly bullish. Therefore, as you approach your goal, you should consider carefully a decision to move your money into safer investments.

Projecting Future Costs

While it is easy to find out how much an item costs today, it takes some calculation to determine what it will cost in five, ten or twenty years. Whether you need to know the future cost of a car, a home, a college education, or retirement, you must first determine what it costs today. Once you know the present cost, you can increase it by a projected rate of inflation to calculate the future cost. For instance, if a one-year college education costs $6,000 today and the projected rate of inflation is 6% per year, you will need to increase the $6,000 beginning cost by 6% per year.

To accomplish this, you must first change the rate of increase into a conversion factor (see Module 2). In our example the conversion factor is 1.06 (6 ÷ 100 +1). The conversion factor is applied to the beginning cost and then to each subsequent year's increasing cost until you reach the year for which you want to project the cost. For example, if you need to know the cost in the year 2000 of a one-year college education that costs $6,000 in 1995, you would multiply $6,000 by 1.06 five times, which would equal $8,029, as shown in Table 9.22.

Table 9.22 *Future Costs*

1995	$6,000 x 1.06 =
1996	$6,360 x 1.06 =
1997	$6,742 x 1.06 =
1998	$7,146 x 1.06 =
1999	$7,575 x 1.06 =
2000	$8,029

In this way, you can calculate the future costs for the years 2001–2003 to determine the four-year cost of a college education beginning in the year 2000: $8,511 in 2001 ($8,029 x 1.06), $9,022 in 2002 ($8,511 x 1.06) and $9,563 in 2003 ($9,022 x 1.06) for a total of $35,125 for the four-year period. Thus, once you know the cost of any item in today's dollars, simply increase it by the projected rate of inflation to calculate its cost in the future.

Savings Needed to Reach a Financial Goal

In Module 6, "Designing a Financial Plan," we used the five-step economic model profile to project target income and savings goals. After we project the amount of raw savings (savings not yet invested), we must then calculate how much savings to invest *monthly* to reach a specific financial goal. This requires knowing both the time frame available to invest and the after-tax rate of return we can expect to earn on the investment. Table 9.23 shows the amount you will need to save monthly for each $1,000 you require to meet a future financial goal, based on the given number of years you have available to save and the after-tax rate of return you project you will earn.

Table 9.23 *Monthly Savings per Thousand*

Years	After-Tax Return 2%	4%	6%	8%	10%	12%	14%	16%
2	$40.88	$40.12	$39.38	$38.67	$37.97	$37.30	$36.65	$36.01
4	20.04	19.27	18.54	17.85	17.18	16.54	15.94	15.35
6	13.09	12.34	11.63	10.96	10.34	9.74	9.19	8.66
8	9.62	8.88	8.20	7.56	6.97	6.43	5.93	5.46
10	7.54	6.82	6.15	5.55	5.00	4.51	4.06	3.65
12	6.16	5.45	4.81	4.24	3.73	3.28	2.88	2.52
14	5.17	4.47	3.86	3.32	2.85	2.44	2.09	1.78
16	4.43	3.75	3.16	2.65	2.22	1.85	1.54	1.28
18	3.86	3.19	2.62	2.15	1.75	1.42	1.15	0.92
20	3.40	2.74	2.21	1.76	1.39	1.10	0.86	0.67
25	2.58	1.97	1.48	1.10	0.81	0.59	0.43	0.31
30	2.04	1.46	1.03	0.71	0.48	0.33	0.22	0.15

Let's look at an example. Suppose a family has two children. One child will start college in ten years, and the second will start college in sixteen years. The amount needed for the first child's education will be $50,000 and the amount needed for the second child's education will be $75,000. Assume that a stock mutual fund will be used as the investment vehicle and that the after-tax rate of return is 8%.

For the first child, the amount the family must save monthly is $277.50; for the second child the requirement is $198.75. We are able to determine this easily by finding the monthly savings amount per thousand at 8% for ten years, which is $5.55, and for sixteen years, which is $2.65. Then we must multiply the savings per thousand amount by the number of thousands of dollars required to determine the total amount of monthly savings needed. In our example, this means multiplying $5.55 by 50 ($50,000 is the cost of the first child's college education), which equals $277.50, and multiplying $2.65 by 75 ($75,000 is the second child's college costs), which equals $198.75. The total amount of savings the family needs to invest over a ten-year period for the first child, therefore, is $33,300 (120 months times $277.50). The total amount of savings the family must invest over a sixteen-year period for the second child is $38,160 (192 months times $198.75).

If the number of years to reach your financial goal or the after-tax rate of return is not shown in this table, simply estimate the monthly payment amount. For example, the monthly savings amount for three years at a 2% after-tax rate of return would be $30.46 (the average of $40.88 and $20.04, the monthly savings amounts for an after-tax rate of return of 2% for two and four years).

If you had a beginning amount of savings on hand today which could be used to meet a future financial goal, you would *first* project what this amount would increase to at the time it was needed. After this was determined you would then begin saving for the *difference* between the future cost of your financial goal and the projected value of your present savings.

For instance, referring to our example of the cost of a college education for the first child which is ten years in the future and costs $50,000–assume that you have $10,000 today. That $10,000 amount would grow to $21,589 in ten years at an 8% after tax return–the return to be earned on the stock mutual fund ($10,800 at the end of year 1: $10,000 x 1.08, $11,664 at the end of year 2: $10,800 x 1.08, and so on to $21,589 at the end of year 10). Therefore what you would need to begin saving for today is $28,411, the difference between $50,000 (the future college cost) and $21,589 (the projected value of your present savings in ten years).

If you rounded the $28,411 to $29,000 and assumed an 8% after tax rate of return for the next ten years on your investment, the savings per thousand needed would be $5.55. Multiplying this amount by 29 (the number of thousands) equals the monthly savings amount required of $160.95.

Advancing the Date of Funding

Throughout your life cycle, you will continually be faced with saving for financial goals. Because some goals require long periods of time in which to save – saving for college and retirement costs, for example – in many instances there can be an overlap in funding.

Generally speaking, after you establish an emergency fund and purchase a home, savings can be targeted toward future college costs, retirement, or both (exclude planned expenditures for the moment). If you are saving for both of these goals simultaneously, however, there is a possibility that both may end up underfunded.

To help alleviate the problems of funding two goals simultaneously over long periods of time, you can begin to fund one financial goal earlier, assuming that savings are available. By starting to save for a college education at the birth of your child – or perhaps even earlier – there will come a time when you will no longer need to add savings to the cumulative amount invested. This is because the principal amount of the investment will grow to the point that, if left invested, it will increase to the necessary future amount you need.

For example, if a child will enter college in five years and $50,000 will be needed to fund the four-year cost, if the child's parents invest $34,000 now and earn 8% after taxes, in five years this amount will grow to approximately $50,000 ($34,000 x 1.08 x 1.08 x 1.08 x 1.08 x 1.08) – note that you can divide (by 1.08 in our example) to work backwards (from $50,000 to $34,000). In this example, therefore, the goal would be to save $34,000 five years before the family actually needs it. They could then leave the money invested and reach their goal without adding further savings (assuming an 8% after-tax rate of return is consistently achieved).

This concept of advancing the funding of one financial goal would then allow funding a second goal to start sooner – retirement, for example. This in turn, could lead to building enough savings prior to retirement so that the principal amount if left invested would reach the amount needed at retirement without further additions. In summary, then, by estimating the amount of money you will need at some future point, you can calculate how much to save now to reach a target amount that will subsequently grow to your desired future value. Once you know the target amount, you can begin saving monthly for it at an assumed after-tax rate of return.

Retirement Planning

Because of advances in health care, many people are living well into their seventies and eighties. As a result, adequate preparation for retirement only makes sense. When planning for retirement there are three primary sources of income from which to draw:

(1) Social security income;

(2) Pension income; and

(3) Income and principal payments generated from personal savings.

The best way to approach retirement planning is first to determine your retirement income needs. This may take some time, as income needs are based on your living costs, which typically change at retirement. (See the living costs schedule in Appendix B to help you calculate your retirement requirements.)

Once you know these amounts, the next step is to estimate the income you would receive from social security, your pension, and personal savings as *if you were age 65 and retiring today*. This approach may take some estimating and assumes that you have made the required payments into social security during your working lifetime and that you have been contributing regularly to your pension. Moreover, this approach will involve contacting the social security office (800-772-1213) and, most likely, your employer for pension information. It will also require determining the amount of personal savings you expect to have and what you can earn on those savings. After you have calculated your retirement sources of income in today's dollars and what your retirement living costs would be in today's dollars, you then need to inflation adjust your retirement income sources and retirement living costs. This is done by increasing today's amounts to future amounts (to the year of your anticipated retirement). This will require estimating an average rate of inflation and then increasing today's dollar amounts by the inflation rate as a conversion factor. A good long-term average rate of inflation to use is 4% (a conversion factor of 1.04) – the average rate for the period 1949-1994 rounded to the nearest whole number.

We recommend that all married individuals prepare three retirement scenarios. The first is a joint-income-and-living-cost scenario for the husband and wife, the second and third are individual retirement scenarios, one for the husband and one for the wife. (If you are a single retiree, you need to prepare only one scenario.)

What you will notice is that the social security payments and pension payments will differ under each scenario. This is because both social security and pension plans offer different options that can or cannot involve payments to a spouse. Pension payments made to a husband and wife (called joint-and-survivor payments) are usually less than payments made to one individual. Because they are indexed for inflation, social security payments generally increase each year, while pension payments are usually fixed.

You will probably need to use personal savings to supplement income from social security and your pension. These savings should be placed in some type of income-producing investment that provides payments of income, and principal if necessary, based on your expected period of retirement.

Table 9.24 *Retirement Scenario*

Year	Age	Social Security Income	Pension Income	Bond Payments (p + i)	Total Retirement Income	Living Costs	Excess/ Shortfall
1995	**65**	$16,600	$8,000	$8,610	$33,210	$31,000	$2,210
1996	**66**	17,264	8,000	8,687	33,951	32,240	1,711
1997	**67**	17,955	8,000	8,825	34,780	33,530	1,250
1998	**68**	18,673	8,000	8,928	35,601	34,871	730
1999	**69**	19,420	8,000	8,998	36,418	36,266	152
2000	**70**	20,585	8,000	9,028	37,613	38,442	-829
2001	**71**	21,820	8,000	9,005	38,825	40,749	-1,924
2002	**72**	23,129	8,000	8,908	40,037	43,194	-3,157
2003	**73**	24,517	8,000	8,731	41,248	45,786	-4,538
2004	**74**	25,988	8,000	8,461	42,449	48,533	-6,084
2005	**75**	27,547	8,000	8,089	43,636	51,445	-7,809

Excesses increase the bond portfolio (and thus the payments) and shortfalls decrease the bond portfolio (and thus the payments).

Table 9.24 lists the sources of income and expenses for a retired couple for the period from 1995 to 2005. In this table, we'll assume that inflation is 4% for the years 1995–1999 and increases to 6% thereafter. We will also assume that living costs increase with the rate of inflation. As far as sources of income go, we'll assume that social security increases with inflation, while the pension income is fixed. Finally, we'll assume that bond payments are based on personal savings of $123,000 invested in a portfolio of bonds that earns 7% after taxes.

In our example, beginning bond payments will consist only of interest (i) through the year 2000, and they will increase annually as excess income is used to purchase more bonds. It is not until the year 2001 that bond payments will include principal (p) to meet the shortfall in living costs first experienced in 2000. Once bond principal starts to be paid out, less interest will be earned each year.

Because pension income is fixed and bond payments start declining in 2001, inflationary increases in living costs begin to overtake the limited increases in income sources. *It is this type of scenario that you must guard against by ensuring that income sources keep pace with inflation.*

Saving for Retirement

As we discussed earlier, saving for retirement is usually accomplished through payment into the federal government's social security system, employer-sponsored retirement savings programs, and personal savings. Many employers offer matching programs – 401(k) and 403(b) – whereby they will match your retirement contributions on a percentage basis up to a ceiling amount.

As a standard rule, after making the required payment into social security, you should try to reach your retirement goals first by using your employer-sponsored program and then by investing your personal savings. The employer-sponsored route is recommended first because, as we mentioned above, matching programs are frequently offered. Moreover, the investment is tax deferred. Self-employed individuals can make use of self-directed retirement programs known as SEPS (simplified employee pensions).

Personal retirement savings plans can be funded using a variety of taxable or tax-deferred investment vehicles in conjunction with an individual retirement account (IRA), subject to limitations (as defined each year in the Form 1040 instruction booklet). The most important part of your retirement program, aside from social security, is understanding the investments that comprise your portfolio. In all cases, you should strive for a well-balanced portfolio using mutual funds, and you should match your risk tolerance to the risk level of the investment.

Preparing a Statement of Financial Position

A properly designed financial plan should include a statement of financial position. Think of this statement as a snapshot—in numerical form—of everything you own (assets), everything you owe (liabilities), and the difference between the two (net worth). Table 9.25 is a statement of financial position for a married couple as of December 31, 1995.

Table 9.25 *Statement of Financial Position*

Assets	Title	Amount	%	Liabilities	Debtor	Amount	%
Cash/Cash Equivalents				Credit Card Balance	Joint	$ 300	1%
Checking Account	Joint	$ 1,000	0%	Car Loan	Husband	$ 8,895	4%
Money Market Fund	Joint	$ 20,000	10%	Car Loan	Wife	$ 8,452	4%
Life Insurance Cash Value	Husband	$ 500	0%	School Loan	Husband	$ 10,000	5%
Certificates of Deposit	Joint	$ 3,000	2%	School Loan	Wife	$ 15,000	8%
				Mortgage	Joint	$ 93,750	46%
Total Cash/ Cash Equivalents		**$ 24,500**	**12%**	**Total Liabilities**		**$136,397**	**68%**
Investment Assets							
Stock	Joint	$ 2,000	1%				
Total Investment Assets		**$ 2,000**	**1%**	**Net Worth**		**$ 63,103**	**32%**
Other Assets							
Residence	Joint	$ 125,000	62%				
Automobile	Husband	$ 15,000	8%				
Automobile	Wife	$ 13,000	7%				
Personal Property	Joint	$ 15,000	7%				
Real Estate–Recreation	Joint	$ 5,000	3%				
Total Other Assets		**$173,000**	**87%**				
Total Assets		**$199,500**	**100%**	**Total Liabilities and Net Worth**		**$199,500**	**100%**

Property is titled jointly and individually, and the statement indicates the dollar amount of each asset and the percentage amount it represents of total assets on the left side and the amount of each debt and its percentage of total liabilities and net worth (which equals total assets) on the right side. The difference between total assets and total liabilities is the couple's net worth.

Total assets equals total liabilities plus net worth. This is the beginning equation from which all accounting proceeds. If you think about it for a moment, everything you own is either paid for or has some debt associated with it. Everything *owned* is represented by total assets. The portion owed is represented by total liabilities. The difference is *net worth* (ownership dollars minus debt dollars).

Our couple's joint personal balance sheet lists total assets of $199,500. Debts total $136,397, yielding a net worth of $63,103. Note that total liabilities of $136,397 and net worth of $63,103 equal total assets of $199,500. Total assets are broken down into three main categories: (1) cash and cash equivalents, (2) investment assets, and (3) other assets.

Cash and Cash Equivalents

Cash and cash equivalents are either cash items or items that can be turned immediately into cash without loss. These assets include certificates of deposit, even though CDs have set maturity schedules and carry a penalty for early withdrawal. Table 9.25 shows that our couple has $1,000 in a non-interest-bearing checking account (titled jointly), $20,000 in a money market account (titled jointly), $500 of cash value in a $25,000 whole life insurance policy (titled in the husband's name with wife as beneficiary), and $3,000 in certificates of deposit titled jointly. Cash and cash equivalents equal $24,500, which represents 12% of their total assets of $199,500.

Investment Assets

Our couple's investment assets consist only of stock valued at $2,000 (titled jointly). Stocks, bonds, pension plans, IRAs, limited partnerships, mutual funds, and ownership in businesses are other investment assets. Since each of these investments could involve loss of principal if turned into cash, they are not included in the cash/cash equivalents section of the financial statement.

Our couple's investment assets account for 1% of their total assets.

Other Assets

A residence valued at $125,000 (titled jointly), two automobiles valued at $15,000 and $13,000 (titled separately), personal property of $15,000 (titled jointly), and real estate valued at $5,000 (titled jointly) make up our couple's other assets. These assets total $173,000 and are 87% of the couple's total assets.

Liabilities

Their liabilities consist of the following: a $300 credit card balance (titled jointly), car loan balances of $8,895 and $8,452 (titled separately), college loans of $10,000 and $15,000 (titled separately), and the balance on a thirty-year, 8% mortgage of $93,750 (titled jointly). Total liabilities of $136,397 are 68% of the couple's total assets. (Note that school loans, which are a very real liability, have no corresponding asset to be matched against. This is because education is an intangible asset that does not appear on a balance sheet.)

Net Worth

Our couple's net worth is $63,103 (total assets of $199,500 minus total liabilities of $136,397), or 32% of their total assets.

Statement of Income and Expense

The next statement to prepare is the statement of income and expense. This statement follows the format of the five-step economic model—that is, it begins with gross income and then lists income taxes, after-tax income, living costs, and savings. Table 9.26 is a statement of income and expense for our young, married couple where one spouse works full-time and the other works part-time.

Table 9.26 *Statement of Income and Expense*

Year (December 31)	1995	%		5-Step Economic Model
Inflows				
Gross Income (Husband)	$ 28,000	63%		Gross Income (1)
Gross Income (Wife)	$ 15,629	35		
Interest Income (Joint)	$ 690	1.5		
Dividend Income (Joint)	$ 125	0.5		
Total Inflows	**$44,444**	**100%**		
Outflows				
Income Taxes	**$ 8,889**	**20%**		**Incomes Taxes (2)**
After-Tax Income	**$35,555**	**80%**	**100%**	**After-Tax Income (3) 1–2 or 4+5**
Living Costs				**Living Costs (4)**
1. Food and Beverages				
Food	$ 3,000	8%		
Subtotal	$ 3,000	8		
2. Housing				
Mortgage and Real Estate Taxes	$ 11,844	34		
Utilities/Household Expenses	$ 1,200	3		
Homeowner's/ Personal Property Insurance	$ 650	2		
Subtotal	$ 13,694	39		
3. Apparel and Upkeep				
Clothing	$ 800	2		
Subtotal	$ 800	2		
4. Transportation				
Auto Loan Payments and Insurance	$ 6,024	17		
Gasoline and Repairs	$ 2,287	6		
Subtotal	$ 8,311	23		
5. Medical Care				
Medical/Dental	$ 300	1		
Subtotal	$ 300	1		
6. Entertainment				
Vacations, Fitness Programs and Videos	$ 1,323	4		
Subtotal	$ 1,323	4		
7. Other Goods and Services				
Personal Care Items	$ 5,127	15		
Subtotal	$ 5,127	15		
Total Living Costs	**$32,555**		**92%**	
Savings	**$ 3,000**		**8%**	**Savings (5)**
Total Outflows	**$44,444**		**100%**	**Total of Steps 2, 4 and 5**

Income taxes (federal, FICA, state, and local) are estimated at 20% of gross income.

When it is used in conjunction with the statement of financial position, the statement of income and expense provides pertinent information for managing a financial plan.

Other Financial Planning Considerations

To conclude, here are three final points you must address to ensure sound financial planning:

(1) Meet regularly with your insurance agents to make sure you maintain adequate insurance for your home or apartment (liability and personal property), personal belongings, and automobiles. Periodically review all health insurance, life insurance, and disability insurance; if you are self-employed, review your professional insurance. Also review all beneficiary designations regularly to make sure they are up-to-date.

(2) Have an attorney draw wills and title property according to the laws of your state. Also contact an attorney or financial planner to discuss estate planning.

(3) Make a conscious effort to follow the monthly rate of inflation, market indexes, and the performance of your investments. Start reading business newspapers and periodicals. Stay informed.

In summary, you can be your own best financial planner. No one cares more about your financial plans; no one wants to reach your financial goals more than you do. No one better understands your tolerance for risk. Use the system…it works. We wish you good fortune as you embark on sound financial planning and begin to *manage your own financial future!*

Appendix A: Detail for Target Annual Living Costs 1996-2000

	1995	1996	1997	1998	1999	2000
	Actual Living Costs	**Target Living Costs**	**Target Living Costs**	**Target Living Costs**	**Target Living Costs**	**Target Living Costs**
Food and Beverages						
Food	$ 4,501	$ 4,614	$ 4,729	$ 4,847	$ 4,968	$ 5,092
Housing						
Mortgage	$ 6,046	$ 6,046	$ 6,046	$ 6,046	$ 6,046	$ 6,046
Real Estate Taxes	2,800	2,870	2,942	3,016	3,091	3,168
Utilities/Household Expenses	1,850	1,896	1,943	1,992	2,042	2,093
Homeowners Insurance	725	743	762	781	801	821
Subtotal	$11,421	$11,555	$11,693	$11,835	$11,980	$12,128
Apparel and Upkeep						
Clothing	$ 1,589	$ 1,629	$ 1,670	$ 1,712	$ 1,755	$ 1,799
Transportation						
Auto Loans	$ 2,450	$ 2,450	$ 2,450	$ 2,450	$ 2,450	$ 2,450
Car Insurance	875	897	919	942	966	990
Gasoline and Repairs	901	924	947	971	995	1,020
Public Transportation	275	282	289	296	303	311
Subtotal	$ 4,501	$ 4,553	$ 4,605	$ 4,659	$ 4,714	$ 4,771
Medical Care						
Medical Costs/Insurance	$ 1,194	$ 1,224	$ 1,255	$ 1,286	$ 1,318	$ 1,351
Dental/Eye Examinations	475	487	499	511	524	537
Prescription Drugs	185	190	195	200	205	210
Subtotal	$ 1,854	$ 1,901	$ 1,949	$ 1,997	$ 2,047	$ 2,098
Entertainment						
Vacations	$ 559	$ 573	$ 587	$ 602	$ 617	$ 632
Fitness Programs	375	384	394	404	414	424
Video Rentals	125	128	131	134	137	140
Subtotal	$ 1,059	$ 1,085	$ 1,112	$ 1,140	$ 1,168	$ 1,196
Other Goods and Services						
Life Insurance	$ 500	$ 513	$ 526	$ 539	$ 552	$ 566
Credit Card Debt	50	50	50	50	50	50
Charitable Giving	125	128	131	134	137	140
Personal Care Items	879	901	924	947	971	995
Subtotal	$ 1,554	$ 1,592	$ 1,631	$ 1,670	$ 1,710	$ 1,751
Total Living Costs	$26,479	$26,929	$27,389	$27,860	$28,342	$28,835

Appendix B: Five-Step Economic Model Profile

	Step 1			Step 2			Step 3		
Year	Actual Gross Income	Target Gross Income	Actual Minus Target	Actual Income Taxes	Target Income Taxes	Actual Minus Target	Actual After-Tax Income	Target After-Tax Income	Actual Minus Target
Base									
Total									

	Step 4			Step 5		
Year	Actual Living Costs	Target Living Costs	Actual Minus Target	Actual Savings	Target Savings	Actual Minus Target
Base						
Total						

Appendix B: Living Costs Schedule

	Base Year Actual Living Costs	Actual Living Costs	Target Living Costs	Actual Minus Target
Food and Beverages				
Housing				
Apparel and Upkeep				
Transportation				
Medical Care				
Entertainment				
Other Goods and Services				
Total Living Costs				

Appendix C: Annual Savings Rates, 1949-1994

Year	Percent	Year	Percent
1949	3.7 %	1972	7.0%
1950	5.9	1973	9.0
1951	7.3	1974	8.9
1952	7.2	1975	8.7
1953	7.0	1976	7.4
1954	6.2	1977	6.3
1955	5.7	1978	6.9
1956	7.1	1979	7.0
1957	7.2	1980	7.9
1958	7.4	1981	8.8
1959	6.3	1982	8.6
1960	5.7	1983	6.8
1961	6.6	1984	8.0
1962	6.5	1985	6.4
1963	5.9	1986	6.0
1964	6.9	1987	4.3
1965	7.0	1988	4.4
1966	6.8	1989	4.0
1967	8.1	1990	4.2
1968	7.1	1991	5.0
1969	6.5	1992	5.5
1970	8.0	1993	4.1
1971	8.3	1994	4.1

Appendix D: Sources of Information

Ibbotson Data

Stocks, Bonds, Bills, and Inflation 1995 Yearbook. Ibbotson Associates, 225 North Michigan Avenue, Suite 700, Chicago, IL 60601-7676.

Mutual Fund Data

Investment Company Institute, P.O. Box 66140, Washington, DC 20035-6140.

Value Line Data

Value Line Publishing Inc., 711 Third Avenue, New York, NY 10017-4064.

Other Financial Data as noted

The Wall Street Journal, New York, NY, 17 March 1995 and 17 November 1995.

Government Publications

Please note: Publications printed by the Government Printing Office can be purchased at, or ordered through, your local federal government bookstore. To find the address and phone number for the federal government bookstore nearest you, refer to the "Government Offices - United States" section in your local phone directory and look for the listing for "General Services Administration, Government Printing Office Bookstore."

Consumer Price Index Readings 1949-1994

U.S. Department of Labor, Bureau of Labor Statistics. Consumer Price Index Readings 1949-1994. Washington, D.C.

CPI Product Groups and Percentage Weightings

U.S. Department of Labor, Bureau of Labor Statistics. BLS Handbook of Methods (Chapter 19, The Consumer Price Index). Washington, D.C.

Economic Report of the President. Washington, D.C.: U.S. Government Printing Office, Superintendent of Documents, Mail Stop: SSOP, Washington, DC 20402-9328.

Family Income Ranges

Current Population Reports, Consumer Income, Series P60. U.S. Department of Commerce, U.S. Bureau of The Census, Income Statistics Branch/HHES Division. Washington, D.C. 20233-8500. (under development, but unpublished, as of the printing of this book).

Federal Tax Information

U.S. Department of the Treasury, Internal Revenue Service. 1995 Form 1040 and Instruction Booklet. Bloomington, IL. Call 1-800-829-3676 to order this form and instruction booklet.

Median Family Incomes

Current Population Reports, Series P60. U.S. Department of Commerce, U.S. Bureau of the Census, Income Statistics Branch/HHES Division. Washington, DC 20233-8500.

Single Family Home Prices

New Single Family Homes Prices: 1963-1994. U.S. Department of Housing and Urban Development, 451 Seventh Street, SW, Washington, DC 20410.

Private College Costs

Private College Costs 1964-1994. U.S. Department of Education, 600 Independence Avenue, SW, Washington, DC 20202.

Index

A

B

C

D

E

F

G

H

I

L

M

N

O

P

R

S

T

U

Notes:

Notes:

Notes:

Notes: